W9-BUI-925

THE BEST IS STILL TO COME . . .

What's the biggest crime committed by transvestites?

Male fraud.

What do you get when you mix marijuana with an aphrodisiac?

Tumbleweed.

What company is the leading manufacturer of vibrators?

Genital Electric.

IN *TOTALLY GROSS JOKES!*

BESTSELLERS FOR EVERYONE!

GROSS JOKES (1244, $2.50)
by Julius Alvin
You haven't read at all—until you read GROSS JOKES! This complete compilation is guaranteed to deliver the sickest, sassiest laughs!

TOTALLY GROSS JOKES (1333, $2.50)
by Alvin Julius
From the tasteless ridiculous to the taboo sublime, TOTALLY GROSS JOKES has enough laughs in store for even *the most* particular humor fanatics.

MUNICH 10 (1300, $3.95)
by Lewis Orde
They've killed her lover, and they've kidnapped her son. Now the world-famous actress is swept into a maelstrom of international intrigue and bone-chilling suspense—and the only man who can help her pursue her enemies is a complete stranger. . . .

PAY THE PRICE (1234, $3.95)
by Igor Cassini
Christina was every woman's envy and every man's dream. And she was compulsively driven to making it—to the top of the modeling world and to the most powerful peaks of success, where an empire was hers for the taking, if she was willing to PAY THE PRICE.

Available wherever paperbacks are sold, or order direct from the Publisher. Send cover price plus 50¢ per copy for mailing and handling to Zebra Books, 475 Park Avenue South, New York, N.Y. 10016. DO NOT SEND CASH.

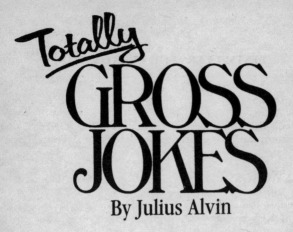

Totally GROSS JOKES

By Julius Alvin

ZEBRA BOOKS
KENSINGTON PUBLISHING CORP.

ZEBRA BOOKS

are published by

KENSINGTON PUBLISHING CORP.
475 Park Avenue South
New York, N.Y. 10016

Copyright © 1983 by Thomas L. Biracree

All rights reserved. No part of this book may be reproduced in any form or by any means without the prior written consent of the Publisher, excepting brief quotes used in reviews.

Printed in the United States of America

To Nancy, who's been totally patient, totally understanding, and totally loving. Now you can open your eyes and take your hands away from your ears.

CONTENTS

Chapter One:

MORE REVOLTING RACIAL AND ETHNIC JOKES

What did the Mexican man and the Polish girl call their baby?

Retardo.

What's the difference between Scotch tape and Mexican tape?

Mexican tape doesn't have a sticky side.

What is the name of the Puerto Rican version of "Roots?"

"Weeds."

Why wasn't Christ born in Puerto Rico?

They couldn't find three wise men and a virgin.

Why are there so few blacks in Alaska?

Because the growing season is too short for watermelon.

How can you stop blacks from jumping up and down on the bed?

Put Velcro on the ceiling.

How do you keep five black guys from raping a white woman?

Throw them a basketball.

A moment or two after a highway accident, an old Jewish man came up to a woman lying by the roadside. "Have the police come yet?" the man asked.

"No," the woman moaned.

"Has the ambulance been here yet?"

"No," the injured woman repeated.

"How about the insurance company?"

"No."

"Listen," the Jewish man said, bending down. "Do you mind if I lay down next to you?"

What's an Irish seven course dinner?

A boiled potato and a six pack.

Two Polish hunters managed to kill a deer. They started to drag it back to their truck by the hind legs, but the antlers continually got stuck in the weeds, making their job very difficult. It took them hours to get within a couple hundred yards of the road, where they met a third hunter.

"Hey," the third hunter said, "it's a lot easier if you drag the deer by the antlers."

The two Polacks took the advice. A while later, one said to the other, "That hunter was right. This is a lot easier."

"Yeah," replied his partner. "But now we're over a mile from the truck!"

A barnstorming pilot was touring Scotland selling rides in his open-cockpit bi-plane. One day he got into an argument with a stubborn Scot who insisted that he be allowed to bring his wife along at no extra charge. Finally, the pilot said, "I'll take you up for the price of one if you promise not to utter a sound. One peep, and the price is double."

The pilot and the couple climbed aboard. The pilot executed some death-defying stunts but the Scot and his wife remained totally silent. Finally, the pilot gave up and landed the plane.

"I don't believe it," the pilot called back as he taxied to a halt. "You're a very brave man."

"Thank ye," the Scot replied. "But I can't deny there was one time when you almost had me."

"When was that?"

"When my wife fell out."

A man walked into the bar. As he waited for his drink, he noticed a gorgeous young Indian girl sipping a soft drink at the other end of the bar. He told the bartender to give her a real drink. The bartender replied, "I can't. The C.P. would be on my ass."

"What's the C.P.?"

"City Police."

The man finished his drink and ordered another. Again, he asked the bartender to give the Indian girl a real drink, but this time the bartender said, "I can't. The S.P. would shut me down."

"What's the S.P.?"

"State Police."

Just then the Indian girl got up and walked out of the bar. The man hurried out after her. An hour later, he staggered back into the bar, his clothes covered with blood, his nose broken.

"The F.B.I. got me!" the man moaned.

"What do you mean, the F.B.I.?" the bartender asked.

"A Fucking Big Indian!"

What's the ultimate Jewish dilemma?

Free bacon.

Why won't a JAP eat soybeans?

Because it's a meat substitute.

Did you hear about the JAP who'd been asked to get married several times?

By her mother and father.

How does a JAP eat a banana?

Under duress.

Why do JAPs wear gold diaphragms?

Because their husbands like coming into money.

After temple one evening, two movie producers went to the men's room together. While standing next to each other at the urinal, one asked the other if he knew old Rabbi Rabinowitz.

"Why, yes," the other replied.

"I thought so. He cuts at an angle and you're peeing on my shoe."

What do you call a Puerto Rican driving a Rolls Royce?

A car thief.

What does a JAP mother say to her baby?

Gucci, Gucci.

Why are Jewish children rude?

Heredity.

What's the definition of a modern JAP mother?

One who can hold a safety pin and a sip of Perrier in her mouth at the same time.

Why don't JAPs breast feed their male children?

Because they don't want them to become leeches like their husbands.

How can you tell a disadvantaged Jewish teenager?

He's the one driving a domestic automobile.

What did the JAP make for dinner?

Reservations.

The Russian couple's sex life was terrible, so they went out and bought a black market copy of a sex manual. A week later, the man said to the woman, "Honey, I want to eat your pussy like it says in the book, but it smells so bad. Why don't you go out and buy some of that feminine deodorant spray?"

She agreed. An hour later, she returned, all excited.

"You should see the flavors they have," she told her husband. "Strawberry, cherry, banana. . . ."

"What did you get?" he interrupted.

"Tuna," she replied.

Why did the Southern redneck buy two CB radios?

So he could talk to himself.

The Polish girl told her mother that she was pregnant.

"Are you sure it's yours?" the mother asked.

Why can't Polish farmers raise chickens?

They plant the eggs too deep.

What's the favorite Polish houseplant?

Crabgrass.

A man ran up to the Polish policeman and yelled, "Somebody stole my car!"

"I know," the Polish cop said. "But don't worry. I got the license number."

Why have all dogs been banned from the Vatican?

Because they piss on Poles.

Why can't Poland field an ice-hockey team?

Everyone drowns in spring training.

What's the best selling underarm deodorant in Puerto Rico?

Raid.

Why do Mexicans eat beans for dinner?

So later on in the evening they can take bubble baths.

Why do Puerto Rican dogs have snubbed noses?

From chasing parked cars.

Two Mexicans bought a Country Squire station wagon with wooden sides. When they got it home, they tore off all the wood paneling. They looked at it for a while, then one turned to the other and said, "You know, I liked it better in the box."

Why does it take seven people to give a redneck a shower?

Three to hold him down and four to spit on him.

What's a hoola hoop?

A teething ring for Africans.

Why do blacks go around with their flys open?

In case they have to count to eleven.

How did the first 10,000 slaves come over from Africa?

The first one swam, and the rest crossed by walking on the dead fish.

Why don't they have any sandboxes in Harlem playgrounds?

Because cats kept burying the black kids.

A girl sat sobbing in the police station. "I . . . I was raped by an Irishman," she wailed.

"How do you know it was an Irishman?" the detective asked.

"I had to help him," the girl replied.

How can you tell the mother-in-law at a Jewish wedding?

She's the one down on her knees picking up the rice.

A man went to the doctor and said, "Doc, I'm madly in love with this Polish girl. You've got to help me become a Polack."

"Are you sure?" the doctor said. "In order to do that, we've got to surgically remove half your brain."

The man said that he wanted to go ahead anyway. After the operation, though, the man woke up to find his doctor standing beside his bed. "I'm terribly sorry," the doctor said. "We made a bad mistake. We removed three quarters of your brain."

"Oh, mama mia!" the man cried.

Why did the Polack cry when he stepped in a pile of cow dung?

He thought he was melting.

Why did the Polish airliner crash?

It ran out of coal.

What happened when they dropped the atomic bomb on Warsaw?

It did $10.15 worth of damage.

Did you hear about the Southern redneck?

He was so lazy that he married a pregnant woman.

How are redneck children taught to put on their underwear?

Yellow in front, brown behind.

The barefoot Southern hillbilly woman walked into the doctor's office and complained, "Those dang birth control pills y'all gave me don't work."

"What do you mean?" the physician asked. "Have you been taking them every day?"

"Yep," the girl said defiantly. "But the dang things keep falling out."

The WASP husband came home to find his new wife in tears. "Muffy, what's the matter?" he asked.

She replied, "I wanted to fix you a nice martini. I started out by rinsing off the ice cubes in hot water, and now I can't find them."

Why are rectal thermometers banned in Poland?

They cause too much brain damage.

What is the dirtiest four letter word in Harlem?

Work.

Why won't there ever be an Italian president?

They'll never find enough plastic slip covers for the furniture in the White House.

What do you get when you cross an Italian and a gorilla?

A moron who doesn't have to wear winter underwear.

Did you hear about the Italian businessman who went broke?

He imported 250,000 cans of underarm deodorant to Italy and didn't sell a single one.

How do Italians count?

1, 2, 3, 4, 5, another, another, another.

Why do Italians and Jews get along?

Because Italians invented the toilet seat and Jews invented the hole.

Jose was sitting as usual, his back leaning against the adobe wall of his friend Pedro's shack. Then Pedro came out of the shack with a butterfly in his hand.

"Ay Pedro," Jose called, "where are you going with the butterfly?"

"I'm going to get some butter."

"You're an idiot," Jose scoffed. "Butter doesn't come from butterflies."

But a few minutes later, to Jose's astonishment, Pedro returned with a pot of butter.

The next day, Pedro hurried out with a jar of horseflies.

"Where are you going?" Jose asked.

"To get horses," Pedro said.

Jose couldn't stop laughing—until Pedro came back an hour later leading two beautiful stallions.

The next day, Jose saw Pedro walking out of his shack carrying a handful of weeds. "What's that?" he called out.

"Pussy willow," Pedro answered.

"Hold on!" Jose roared, leaping to his feet. "I'm coming with you!"

What do they call Toys-R-Us in Harlem?

We-B-Toys.

Why can't Italians take showers?

Because oil and water don't mix.

What's the difference between Italian starlets and French starlets?

French starlets don't have mustaches.

Why did the Polack lose his job as an elevator operator?

He couldn't learn the route.

Why did the people at the World's Fair run around looking for manhole covers?

They were looking for the entrance to the Polish Pavilion.

Why couldn't the Russian woman get out of bed in the morning?

She was so fat she kept rocking herself back to sleep.

What do Russian women use as garters?

Inner tubes.

Why don't they allow Puerto Ricans to swim in the Hudson River?

Because they'd leave a ring on the shore.

What's the first lesson you learn at a Puerto Rican driving school?

How to open a locked car with a coat hanger.

What's the difference between a hippopotamus and a Russian mother-in-law?

Less than fifty pounds.

The Irish girl finally got her fiance to the altar two weeks before Easter. On their wedding night, she put on a very short, sexy nightgown and crawled into bed. But her husband didn't respond.

"What's wrong?" she asked.

"I . . . I can't make love," he answered. "It's Lent."

"Lent?" she shouted. "To whom and for how long?"

The WASP couple were making love when the man suddenly stopped and asked in a very concerned voice, "Darling, am I hurting you?"

"No. Why did you ask?"

"Because you moved."

What do you call an Italian that marries a Negro?

A social climber.

How do you tell the bride at a hillbilly wedding?

She's the one that's pregnant.

Did you hear about the hillbilly who believed in long engagements?

His girlfriend was pregnant six months before he married her.

The redneck farmer was disturbed when he found his son masturbating several times a day. "Boy, you got to stop that," he said. "Go out and get yourself a wife."

So the boy went out, and soon he found a pretty young girl, whom he married. But a week or so after the wedding, the farmer found his son whacking off again. "You crazy, boy?" the father yelled. "That Lucy Mae's a fine girl."

"I know, Pop," the boy said, "but her arm gets awful tired sometimes."

Why doesn't the Navy let Italians join underwater demolition teams?

Because they keep leaving oil slicks.

How do you train Arabs to be soldiers?

First you teach them to put their hands up.

A Polack walked into a bar with a frog on his head.

"Where did you get that?" the startled bartender asked.

"Well," the frog replied, "it started out as a wart on my ass."

Why did the Irishwoman think her husband was unfaithful?

None of the children looked like him.

Why did the Polish housewife get rid of her freezer?

She got tired of cutting the ice into little squares to fit into the trays.

What did the Polack do when he found out he was promoted from second to third grade?

He got so excited he cut himself shaving.

What did the redneck father do when the guy said he wanted to marry his daughter?

He was so surprised, the gun fell right out of his hands.

A Scot went into a whore house and announced he could spend no more than ten dollars. The madam told him that the cheapest rate was twenty dollars. After a monumental argument, the madam coaxed the money out of the tightfisted man and sent him upstairs with a girl.

The girl undressed and pulled the Scot down on her, but to her amazement the man started to fuck her navel. "That's not the place," the girl barked. "My hole is further down."

"For twenty dollars," the Scot replied, "I want a hole of my own."

How can you tell a cultured Polish male?

He makes sure to take the dishes out of the sink before he pisses in it.

Two black dudes were walking home from their jobs and discussing their wives' spending habits. "Man," one finally exclaimed, "I don't understand how women can spend so much money. Take my wife. I mean, she don't drink, she don't smoke weed, and she's got her *own* pussy!"

A young Polack visited his folks the day after his wedding. His father took him aside and asked, "How did things go last night?"

"Pretty good, Pop," he said. "The way she was acting, I think I could have fucked her."

What's the difference between a Jew and a canoe?

A canoe tips.

A Polish foreign exchange student wrote home to his mother in Warsaw to say that he was going to marry an American girl. The mother wrote back, begging her son to reconsider.

"It's a mistake, son," the mother wrote. "Those American girls are terrible cooks, they can't keep you happy in bed, and they'll call you a dumb Polack whenever they get angry."

The young man ignored his mother's advice, married the girl, then wrote a few weeks later, "Mom, you were wrong. My wife is a wonderful cook, she's terrific in bed, and she doesn't call me a dumb Polack if I don't call her a dirty nigger."

An Italian was sitting at a bar, having a few drinks and chatting with the bartender. The news came on, and the first story showed a man on the ledge of a tall building threatening to jump. The bartender turned to the Italian and said, "I'll bet you ten bucks the guy jumps."

"Okay," the Italian said.

A minute or so later, the man jumped. The Italian fished in his wallet for a ten when the bartender said, "Hey, I can't take your money. I got to tell you I saw this earlier on the news. I knew he was going to jump."

"No, here, take the money," the Italian said. "I saw it before, too, and I didn't think the guy would be so stupid to jump again."

Why aren't there any vampires south of the border?

Every time they suck a Mexican's blood they have the shits for a week.

What's a *wiener?*

The first person across the finish line at a Mexican track meet.

What do you get when you try to cross a Puerto Rican and a pig?

Nothing. There are some things even a pig won't do.

How many Polacks does it take to ice-fish?

Six. Two to cut the hole in the ice and four to push the boat through.

What do black people call the Easter Bunny?

Dinner.

What's foreplay for an Italian?

Whistling.

How do you get three Polacks off a couch?

You jerk one off and the other two come.

Why do blacks carry monkeys on their backs?

For spare parts.

Did you hear about the hillbilly who left his estate in trust for his wife?

She can't touch it until she's thirteen.

The Chinaman started to fart like crazy while he was screwing the prostitute. She finally shouted, "Hey, why are you doing that?"

The Chinaman replied, "My pricky have such a good time, my assy shout Hoolray!"

What's a stingy Scotsman?

One who sleeps with his mother-in-law to save wear and tear on his wife.

The Scotsman went to the whorehouse with ten dollars. After a long argument with the madam, he was finally escorted to the very top of the house to a small, dark room. He groped around in the dark until he found warm flesh, then he pounced. He pumped away, just on the verge of discharging his load, when a very foul odor caused him to gag. "What's that?" he demanded.

"Please, sir," came a feeble voice. "They told me I had to do one more trick, but I'm far too old to come. So I just shit."

A Jewish couple were taking a walk around the zoo when they stopped at the gorilla cage. The gorilla took one look at the woman and began to breathe passionately. With his powerful arms, he spread apart two bars, reached out, grabbed the woman, pulled her into the cage, then pushed her to the floor of the cage and fell on top of her.

"Saul!" the woman shrieked. "What should I do?"

Saul answered calmly, "Do what you always do. Tell him you've got a headache."

On the day before her 12th baby was due, Mrs. Masucci told her husband, "I've had it. You men want more and more children, but now we women have fixed it. We went to church and prayed to the saint to make the fathers share the pain of labor. And from the way the candles flared, I know the saint listened."

Her husband laughed at her for her superstition. Later that night, Mrs. Masucci began to feel the first labor pains. Smugly, her husband touched his stomach. Nothing, not the least twinge. He leaned forward and poured himself another glass of wine.

Then, suddenly, from the street came a terrible scream. The man from next door was clutching his belly and rolling on the sidewalk. . . .

Two Polish farm boys wanted to go to Warsaw to have a good time. Their father gave them permission, but he told them to put on rubbers and not take them off for any reason, so that they wouldn't get any girls in trouble. They went to the city and had a ball.

The next day they were back planting crops. One Polack turned to the other and said, "I don't really care if those girls get pregnant, do you?"

"Naw," the other said.

"Good. Let's take these rubbers off. I've had to pee all day."

The Alabama redneck was inviting guests to his party. One young lady asked if she could bring something.

"Sure," replied the redneck. "Bring a tray of pickled beets, fresh spinach, and yellow squash."

"Gosh," the girl said, "that doesn't sound much like party food."

"Oh, it ain't, honey," the redneck drawled. "But it sure does make purty puke."

An American, an Englishman, and a Scotsman went into a restaurant and ordered soup. Each of the three bowls arrived with a fly in it. When the American found the fly, he took a deep breath, blew it out, and continued eating. The Englishman dipped his fly out politely and continued with his lunch. The Scotsman grabbed the fly, held him over the bowl, and shouted, "Okay, spit it out! All of it!"

What's a fart?

A Greek love call.

A very naive young liberal couple decided they'd like to have a black child. The husband asked the janitor at work how he could get one.

"We get black children the same way white folk do," the janitor said. "We fuck."

So the husband went home, tried the janitor's advice, and nine months later the wife gave birth to a boy—but the baby was white. Feeling he'd done something wrong, he went back and talked to the janitor.

"Does you have a pecker thirteen inches long?" the black man asked.

"No."

"Does you have a pecker four inches thick?"

"No."

"Then dat's the problem," the janitor said. "You's letting too much light in."

What's the definition of "honky-tonk?"

The sound that's made when you hit a white man over the head.

What do you call a black with no arms?

Honest.

Why do they put a pile of shit in the corner at an Italian wedding?

To keep the flies off the bride.

Why was the Puerto Rican baby called Juan Carlos Jorge Chino Ricardo Tomas Xavier Pedro Manuel Bernardo?

His mother named him for everyone at the gang bang.

What do Mexican men use as cock rings?

Flea collars.

How can you tell a Polish wedding?

The bride's so ugly everyone kisses the groom.

What did the WASP housewife do when she burned the meat?

She put suntan oil on it.

How do Italian parents know when their daughter is old enough to date?

They make her stand up and stretch her arms straight out. If the hair under her armpits reaches the floor, she's old enough.

What are the vital statistics of the winner of the Miss Russia Beauty Contest?

36-24-36. And the other leg is the same.

Why don't Polish women give good head?

Because they can't get their lips all the way over the guy's ears.

Why did the lazy Puerto Rican check into the hospital?

For a hernia transplant, so he wouldn't have to do any more heavy work.

What do you call a Polack with half a brain?

Gifted.

Why was the Polish historian so mad when a thief mugged him and stole his books?

Because he hadn't finished coloring one of them.

What's an "election?"

Something you find on a Chinese blide-gloom.

What's the best selling douche in Poland?

Liquid Plumber.

Why is the average age of a private in the Polish Army 43 years old?

They draft them right out of high school.

A man lying in a hospital bed accidently took a shit. He didn't want the nurses to find out, so he balled up the sheet and threw it out the window. It landed on a Polack who was walking by.

The Polack finally got untangled from the sheet, but he was a mess. Shaken, he walked into a bar and ordered a beer. "Get out of here!" the bartender said. "You smell terrible."

"You would too," the Polack said, "if you'd beat the shit out of a ghost that flew out of the fourth floor window."

What do you call a black woman who takes birth control pills?

A humanitarian.

Why did the black man buy $5,000 worth of Cadillac tires?

Because he wanted his house to have all white walls.

Why don't doctors circumcise blacks any more?

They discovered they were throwing away the best part.

Did you hear about the Polacks who went ice fishing?

They caught two hundred pounds, then drowned trying to fry it.

How do you recognize an Italian airliner?

It has outdoor toilets.

Why do flies have wings?

So they can beat Italians to the garbage cans.

What's the best selling toilet paper in Mississippi?

The brand with instructions printed on every sheet.

How do you recognize a Polack in a department store?

He's the one trying to slam the revolving door.

What's the Polish version of the "seven year itch?"

Crabs.

Why didn't the WASP want his wife to have a baby by artificial insemination?

He didn't like the idea of using other people's leftovers.

Chapter Two:

MORE APPALLING ANIMAL JOKES

Two roosters were talking in the barnyard. The old, wise rooster said to the new rooster, "Let's race. I'll bet you a bushel of corn I can run faster than you."

The new rooster nearly keeled over from laughing, because he knew he was much stronger. He even agreed to give the old rooster a head start. The old rooster took off around the barn and the new rooster began running after him. As the two came around the corner, the farmer raised his gun and shot the new rooster.

"Damn it," the farmer swore. "Third queer rooster I've bought this week."

The rather haughty young girl was strolling through the zoo when she stopped at the monkey cage. Mystified to find the cage empty, she queried the keeper, "Where are the monkeys today?"

"It's mating season," he replied. "They're back in the cave."

"Will they come out if I throw some peanuts?"

"I don't know, lady," the keeper replied. "Would you?"

A performing octopus could play the drums, the piano and the accordian. His trainer, looking for a bigger contract, put a bagpipe in his room.

Hours passed, and the trainer didn't hear a note of music. He reentered the room to find the octopus lying exhausted on the floor. "What's the matter?" he asked. "Can't you play it?"

"Play it?" the octopus replied. "I've been trying to lay it."

A gorilla escaped from his cage and fled the zoo. He broke into a nearby cottage where a young woman lived. Starved for female attention, the animal fell upon her and had his brutal way repeatedly. By the time the keepers and the police arrived, the young woman was comatose.

A week in the hospital healed her physical wounds, but she was distraught. She wouldn't see anybody for weeks. Finally, an old friend came by and said, "You've got to pull yourself together. You've got to get over what happened."

"But he hasn't written," the young woman said tearfully. "He hasn't even called!"

The farmer's son was assigned to bring the prize rooster to the county fair. His father told the young man that if anything happened to the rooster, there'd be hell to pay. The son promised he wouldn't let the rooster out of his sight.

When he got to the fair, however, he was strongly

tempted by the barker for a girly show. He thought for a moment, then decided he'd take the rooster in. He opened the front flap of his overalls, put the rooster inside, and rebuttoned the pants.

Inside the tent, the lights went out and the girls started stripping on stage. A couple was sitting next to the farmer's son. The man was enjoying the show until his girlfriend nudged him and said, "Darling. The man next to me has undone his pants and . . . and his thing is sticking out."

"Don't pay attention," the man said. "You've seen those things before, after all."

"Yeah," the girl replied. "But this one is eating my cracker jacks."

A pair of rabbits was being chased by a pack of hounds when one turned to the other and said, "What are we running for? Why don't we stop and outnumber them?"

"You idiot," the other said. "We have to keep running. We're brothers."

"It won't take long—did it?" the male rabbit said.

Did you hear about the singing canary that fell into the meat grinder?

All week long the family ate shredded tweet.

An easterner went out west to buy a ranch. A friend came out to visit him, and asked the name of the spread.

"We had a terrible time," the new rancher said. "Finally, to settle all the arguments, we called it the Lazy Rocker-Triple W-Diamond Bar-Lucky Sevens Ranch."

"Where are the cattle?" the friend asked.

"None of them survived the branding," the new rancher replied.

A mule kicked a farmer's mother-in-law to death. A huge crowd gathered for the funeral. "That old lady must have been popular," a passer-by remarked.

"Popular, hell," a man replied. "She was the orneriest old lady in the county. These people want to buy the mule that was strong enough to outkick the old bitch."

What did the young doe say as she ran bleeding into the woods?

"That's the last time I do it for ten bucks."

Why did the three little pigs leave home?

Their father was an awful boar.

What do you get when you cross an elephant with a prostitute?

A two-ton pick-up.

What's the ultimate embarrassment for a woman?

Taking her German shepherd to the vet and being told he has the clap.

The man at the bar had drunk so much that the bartender asked him to leave. The customer insisted he wasn't drunk, and he'd prove it. "See that cat coming in the door?" the drunk said. "Well, that cat has only one eye, and that proves I'm not smashed."

"You're drunker than I thought," the bartender said. "That cat isn't coming in the door, he's going out."

The insecticide salesman found himself needing an order so badly that he volunteered to strip naked, spray himself with the product, and spend the night tied to a post in a pasture. The farmer told the man if he didn't get bitten, he'd buy the product.

The next morning the farmer came out to find the salesman utterly exhausted. "Bugs got ya?" the farmer asked.

"No," the salesman replied. "I don't have a bite. But doesn't that calf of yours have a mother?"

Why did the farmer stop screwing his mule?

It was too far around to kiss her.

The two soldiers had been fighting for weeks when they suddenly came upon a lone sheep grazing in a field. "God," one said to the other, "if only that were a woman." The other replied in even more heartfelt tones, "God, if only it were dark."

A bachelor migrated out west and bought a sheep farm outside of a small frontier town where there were no women. After a month he was so horny he went into town and complained to the bartender, who told him, "You'll have to do what the rest of us do. You'll have to make do with a sheep."

The thought sickened the farmer and he returned to his ranch. After another month, however, he couldn't stand it any more. He went back into town, got roaring drunk, then went back out into the night and grabbed the first sheep he could find. It wasn't as bad as he expected, and he rested on the grass for a while before having a second go.

Suddenly, he was awakened by two men grabbing his arms. He felt handcuffs slapped on his wrists and he was wrestled to his feet. He was astounded to see a crowd of angry men around him. He spotted the bartender among them and stunned, asked, "What's wrong? You told me to get a sheep."

"Yeah," the bartender replied. "But, you damn fool, you grabbed the sheriff's girl friend."

The big attraction at the State Fair was a cow reportedly worth a million dollars. "Why is that cow worth so much money?" a curious farmer asked another man standing in line to see the animal.

"Because," the man replied, "if you stand real close, you can see that the cow has a pussy just like a woman's."

The farmer started to roar. The man stared at him until the laughter subsided, then asked, "What's so funny?"

The farmer shook his head, "Just to think, I got a wife with a pussy like a cow's, and she isn't worth a damn cent."

The guy in the sports car told the hitchhiker he could have a ride, but there was no room for his dog. "That's all right," the hitchhiker said. "He'll keep up."

The driver couldn't believe that, but soon he accelerated to 60 mph and sure enough, the dog was keeping pace. The driver stepped on the gas, and the speedometer soon read 80, but the dog was still alongside.

"Damn," the driver said. "What a great dog. I bet you could make a fortune. . . ."

Suddenly, a railroad crossing with flashing red lights loomed up ahead. The driver slammed on the brakes, coming to a stop a few inches from the train.

He and the passenger took a couple of moments to get themselves together. Then they got out. The dog was standing there, wearing a strange red collar.

"What's that red collar for?" the driver asked.

"That's no collar," the hitchhiker said. "He's not used to sudden stops. That's his asshole."

The circus advertised that its lion was the most vicious beast in the world. But when the reporter from the local newspaper arrived to do a story, the beast was calmly sitting in the corner of his cage, licking his private parts. Even when the reporter banged on the bars and yelled, the lion didn't move.

The noise attracted the keeper, who came over to the cage. "You're guilty of false advertising," the reporter said. "This lion's more of a pussycat. He's even licking himself like a cat."

"Licking himself, hell," the keeper said. "He caught hold of the Mexican who cleans up around here and ate him. Now he's just trying to get the greasy taste out of his mouth."

Why did the police arrest the woman who swam the English Channel for cruelty to animals?

She kept her pussy under water for 14 hours.

Chapter Three:

MORE OFFENSIVE JUVENILE JOKES

What was the name of the little boy whose nuts grew every time he told a lie?

Pistachio.

"I have some bad news for you," the grade school principal advised the mother of the twelve year old. "I personally overheard your daughter offering to . . . well . . . offering to do an F word with a boy in her class."

"An F word? But we've told Jennifer never, never to use any four letter words!" the girl's mother protested.

"That means I have some worse news for you," the principal said. "The four letter word she used has nine letters."

A little girl stared with fascination at the pregnant woman sitting on the park bench. Finally, curiosity got the best of her and she went up, pointed to the woman's stomach, and asked, "What's that?"

"That's my own sweet baby," the woman replied.

"Do you love her?" the little girl asked.

"I love her very much," the mother-to-be answered.

The little girl looked at the woman sternly. "Then how come you ate her?"

A young boy went into a liquor store and asked for a bottle of whiskey. The clerk said he couldn't sell it, but the boy insisted it was for his father, who used whiskey as a laxative.

"Well, okay," the clerk said. "As long as it's for medicinal reasons."

Later, the clerk was going home from work when he saw the boy reeling around, drunk. He grabbed the boy and said angrily, "Hey, you told me that whiskey was a laxative for your father."

The boy nodded. "It is. He'll sure shit when he sees me."

The little boy was out in his backyard, turning worms hard as nails with something he applied with an eye dropper. His father came up to him and asked, "Where did you get that stuff?"

"I made it with my chemistry set," the boy replied.

"Make me a batch of it," the father said, "and I'll buy you a new bicycle."

The boy mixed up a batch for his father. A couple

days later he woke up to find two new bicycles in the garage. "Wow," he exclaimed, "you got me two!"

"That's right, son," the father said. "One from me, and one from your mother."

During recess, a little boy slipped on the monkey bars and hurt his crotch. His teacher sent him to the school nurse.

Shortly afterwards, the boy returned to the classroom with his zipper down and his little penis hanging out.

"What are you doing?" the teacher gasped.

The boy replied, "The nurse told me if I could stick it out until noon, I could go home."

A teacher and a student were relieving themselves at a urinal in the school rest room. When the boy zipped up and started straight for the door, the teacher called out, "Didn't your parents teach you to wash your hands after you piss?"

The boy stopped and said, "No. They taught me not to piss on my hands."

A boy came into the playground to find his friend sitting in the corner, shaking like a leaf. "What happened, Billy?" he asked.

Billy said, "I was walking down Main Street when that big bully from the seventh grade started to chase me. I turned down the alley but he slid around the corner after me. Then I ran down Elm and around the corner, but he slid after me again."

"Wow," the second boy said. "If I'd been you, I would have shit in my pants."

"What do you think that bully was sliding on?" Billy asked.

A little boy said, "I wish I had a prick like my big brother's. He has to use four fingers to hold it."

"Well, you're using four fingers," his friend said.

"Yeah, but I'm pissing on three of them," the little boy replied.

One kid was worried about passing his history test. Another kid told him to write the answers in his undershorts. The first kid took the advice, then went into the testing room. He finished the test in such a short time that before the teacher collected the papers, she asked him to answer a few questions aloud.

The first question was, "How many original colonies were there in America?" The kid took a quick look at his shorts to make sure, then said, "Twenty-eight."

"Wrong," the teacher said. The kid was puzzled, but he agreed to answer a second question: "What are the colors of the American flag?" The kid took another look, then said with confidence, "Brown and white."

"Wrong again," the teacher said. The last question was, "Who was the first president of the United States?"

"I know this one's right," the kid said. "J.C. Penny!"

The little boy wandered into the bathroom just as his mother was climbing out of the shower. He stared for a moment at the black triangle between her legs, then pointed and asked, "Mommy, what's that down there?"

The mother stammered for a moment, then said, "Why, darling, that's my black sponge."

The answer seemed to satisfy the little boy. But later in the day, when the mother was in the kitchen, the boy came up to her and asked, "Can I see your black sponge again?"

"No, dear," the mother replied. "I've lost it."

The boy went away. Later, however, he dashed back into the kitchen with a huge grin on his face. "Mommy, Mommy," he yelled. "I've found your black sponge. Mrs. Jones next door is cleaning Daddy's face with it!"

Little Jenny's parents were desperate for a sitter, so when Grandpa Smith next door volunteered, they were happy. Soon after the parents left, Grandpa unbuttoned his pants and said to Jenny, "Honey, I want to show you my magic puppet."

"What's magic about it?"

"Touch it," Grandpa said.

She did, and let out a whoop. "It moves!"

"Yep," Grandpa said. "And that's not all. If you give him some kisses, he'll get bigger and bigger."

Jenny eagerly complied.

An hour later, her parents arrived home to find Jenny in tears and the police on hand. In the distance, they could hear an ambulance siren howling.

"What happened?" the mother asked Jenny.

"We were playing with Grandpa's puppet," the girl

said. "I kept kissing it and it kept getting bigger. Then all of a sudden it spit all over my face. I got so mad I bit its head off."

The precocious nine-year-old girl walked into the house and asked, "Mommy, can I have a baby?"

"No, of course not."

"Are you sure?"

"Positive, darling."

The girl started to run out of the house, shouting, "All right, guys. We can play that same game again."

The young man was beating off as he stood in front of a full length mirror. But try as he would, his member remained totally limp. "Damn," he swore as he finally walked away, "I guess I'm just not my type."

"Would you believe it?" a man groused to his companion at the bar. "My six-year-old son knocked up my secretary."

"That's impossible! How did he do it?"

"The little shit punctured all my rubbers with a pin."

"Mommy," asked the little girl, "does everybody have to have their legs in the air when they go to heaven?"

"No," the mother replied. "Where did you get such a silly idea?"

"Well, I just came from the bedroom. The maid had her legs up in the air and she kept saying, 'God, I'm coming. God, I'm coming.' But Daddy was on top of her and he wouldn't let her up."

The little boy was being a big pest at his parents' bridge party—knocking over glasses, pulling the cards out of people's hands, running through the room, etc. His rather too indulgent mother was unable to get him under control. Finally, an older man said, "Let me have a talk with him."

The man took the boy into another room and returned after ten minutes. Two hours passed and the boy was still quiet as a mouse. When the players changed tables, the mother came up to the man and said, "You're a miracle worker. What in heaven's name did you do to keep him so quiet?"

"Nothing to it," the man said. "I taught him how to masturbate."

What's the definition of "brownie points?"

What you find in a future Girl Scout's training bra.

How did the parents know their son was going to grow up to be a Marine?

They found him in the john reading war comics and beating off.

Chapter Four:

MORE MORTIFYING MEDICAL JOKES

The medical professor asked his class, "What would you do if a child was born without a penis?"

A student replied, "I'd wait until she was sixteen, then give her one."

The psychiatrist was giving his patient a Rorschach test and was amazed to find that the young man associated every ink blot with some bizarre sexual perversion.

"You'd better make another appointment," the psychiatrist said when they finished. "You need a lot of help."

"Fine," the young man said. "But right now I'm more concerned about my date tonight. I want to borrow those dirty pictures."

A man lying on the psychiatrist's couch said, "Doctor, you've got to help me. I'm totally obsessed with making love to a horse."

"A mare or a stallion?" the doctor asked.

The patient glared at the doctor and said icily, "A mare, of course. What do you think I am, a pervert?"

How can you tell an efficient nurse?

She's one that can make a patient without disturbing the bed.

A woman went to the doctor for her annual checkup. When her husband arrived home that evening, he found her standing in front of a mirror, squeezing her tits. "What are you doing?" he asked.

She replied, "The doctor told me I have the breasts of an eighteen-year-old girl."

"But what about your fifty-five-year-old ass?" the man retorted.

She grimaced. "He didn't say anything about you."

The obstetrician came into the waiting room to see the Polack, who was waiting for his wife. "Congratulations," the doctor said. "Your wife is going to have twins."

The Polack's face suddenly turned bright red. He jumped to his feet and started to run out of the office.

The doctor grabbed his arm. "What's wrong?"

"Just wait until I get hold of that other guy," the Polack threatened.

A scientist was testing a machine that manipulated brain waves to raise or lower I.Q. He hired a volunteer who was extremely intelligent and hooked him up. In the middle of the test, however, the doctor got a phone call. When he got back to his patient, the machine registered an I.Q. of 20.

Worried, the doctor turned the machine off and asked the man, "Are you all right?"

The patient looked up with a big, dumb grin on his face and answered, "That's a big ten-four, good buddy."

A man went to his doctor with severe pains in his back and side. After examining him, the doctor said, "I've got some very bad news for you. You've only got twelve hours to live."

"Twelve hours? You've got to be kidding?"

"No," the doctor said. "I couldn't be more serious."

The man rushed home and told his wife. They went to bed and made furious love for hours, finally falling asleep about midnight. At three a.m., the man woke up. Realizing he had only three hours left, he nudged his wife, telling her he wanted to make love again.

She rolled over and groaned, "That's easy for you to say. You don't have to get up in the morning."

What's a psychiatrist?

A man who watches everybody else when a beautiful girl enters the room.

"Doctor," the man said. "I hope you can help me. I'm worried to death about this red ring around my penis."

The doctor had the man drop his pants, then he took a look. After a moment, the physician said, "You've got nothing to worry about, pal. I can fix it."

"How much is it going to cost?"

"Just $20 for this office visit."

"That's great," the patient said. "I visited another specialist who told me I needed a $500 series of injections. How can you cure me for $20?"

"Either the other guy was a quack," the doctor said, "or he doesn't recognize lipstick when he sees it."

A Republican was sitting at a bar with two doctors who were bragging about amazing things being done in medicine. The first said, "Six weeks ago they brought a man in who lost a hand in an accident. I sewed on the hand from a corpse, and now the man's out looking for work."

The second physician said, "I have something even more amazing. Six months ago I implanted a dead man's eyes in a blind woman, and now she's out looking for work."

"That's nothing," the Republican scoffed. "We pulled

off the biggest miracle of all three years ago. We took an asshole out of California and put it in the White House, and now half the country's out looking for work."

A couple took the wrong exit from the expressway and got lost in a dark, deserted ghetto neighborhood. The man drove around until the car ran out of gas. The man decided to get out and walk until he found a gas station.

"Don't leave me!" the woman cried. "Someone could come along and rape me."

"Relax," the man said. "If a man comes along, just tell him we ran out of gas on the way to the V.D. clinic."

Two men were brought into the emergency ward of a hospital late one night. After they had been X-rayed, it was found that they both had fractured skulls.

"Were they in an automobile accident?" asked the doctor.

"No," the nurse replied. "They had a head-on collision at an orgy. They both aimed at the same hole at the same time."

Chapter Five:

MORE INDECENT RELIGIOUS JOKES

The Pope was kidnapped by some Italian terrorists, who told him that in order to be released, he would have to be photographed screwing a fifteen-year-old girl. The terrorists figured that with this hanging over his head, the Pope would stop the Church's campaign against terrorism.

The Pontiff was outraged. But after the terrorists made it clear that he would be killed otherwise, he reluctantly agreed, but only on three conditions. "One," the Holy Father said, "the young girl must be blindfolded so she cannot see what horrible thing is happening. Two, the girl must be wearing ear plugs so she can't hear."

"All right," the leader of the terrorists said. "What's the third condition?"

The Pope replied, "The girl's got to have real big tits."

The young nun rushed into the Mother Superior's office and exclaimed, "We've got a case of syphilis in the convent!"

The Mother Superior looked up and said, "Thank God. I'm sick to death of red wine."

The fundamentalist minister, sorely tempted, finally propositioned the buxom young soprano one evening after choir practice. "Where?" she enthusiastically inquired.

"Maybe . . . maybe right here on the floor," he panted.

"It's too cold," the girl said.

"How about on that bench over there?" the clergyman asked.

"That's way too small," giggled the girl. "But wait, Reverand, how about doing it against the organ standing up?"

"No, no, no," the clergyman cried. "Anybody who came in here, God forbid, they'd think we were dancing."

The Mother Superior of a convent was awakened one night by a lot of commotion. She rushed downstairs to find that one of the young nuns had been raped.

"Be calm, sister," she counseled. "The first thing you must do is eat half a lemon."

"Half a lemon?" queried the young nun. "Will that keep me from getting pregnant?"

"No," the Mother Superior replied. "But it will get rid of that silly grin on your face."

The family doctor, consulted by the hysterical parents of the pregnant teenager, said he positively would not perform an abortion. "But when her time comes," he said, "I'll deliver the baby at a private hospital. Then I'll show it to one of my other patients, say a woman who's married and in for a gall bladder operation. I'll tell her there's been a mistake, it wasn't her gall bladder, she was pregnant and she had a child."

All went as planned, but at the crucial time, there was no available female patient to foist the baby on. There was only a male—a priest. The physician, undaunted, decided to brazen it out. When the priest awakened from the anesthesia, he was informed that, by a miracle, he'd been delivered of a baby boy. Far from being shocked, the cleric was overjoyed at the divine intervention, and raised the boy as his own.

Years later, as the priest lay dying, he concluded that he must unburden his soul to the boy. "I have always told you that I was your father, but that is untrue," he confessed. He told the boy about the miraculous incident at the hospital. "So you see, my boy," the priest announced, "I'm not your father. I'm your mother. The bishop is your father."

The young nun was assigned by the Mother Superior to help old Father Reilly with his Saturday night bath. The next morning, the older nun asked the young girl how it had gone.

"Wonderful!" the nun exclaimed. "I've been assured of eternal salvation."

"How did that happen?"

"Well, Father Reilly took my hand and guided it between his legs. Then a miracle happened, and the key to heaven grew in my hand. Father Reilly said that if the key to heaven fit in my lock, I'd be saved forever."

"Well," the Mother Superior said gruffly, "what did you do?"

"I let Father Reilly put the key to heaven in my lock. It hurt terribly at first, but Father said the pathway to salvation was often painful. And soon the glory of God put me in ecstasy. I didn't know it felt so good to be saved."

"Saved, baloney," the Mother Superior said bitterly. "That Father Reilly is a wicked old devil. For twenty years he's been telling me it was Gabriel's Horn between his legs, and I've been blowing it for all it's worth."

The three young men who wanted to become monks were ushered into the presence of the head abbot. He ordered them to strip naked, saying, "We must make absolutely sure you are immune to the temptations of the flesh before we admit you to our order. That's why Brother Timothy will now tie a bell around the penis of each of you. Then we'll bring in a slut from the village and see who responds."

Brother Timothy accomplished his task, then exited. He returned a few moments later with a gorgeous young blonde whose figure was bursting out of her tight dress. The head abbot ordered her to shed the dress. When her huge silky white tits were revealed, a silver bell began tinkling gently. "Aha," the head abbot cried, pointing to a man on the left. "You're not meant for this order. Pick up your clothes and get out of here."

Crushed, the man obeyed. He turned and bent over. As his ass parted, the two other bells jingled madly.

The Mother Superior got up one morning and decided to make the rounds to see how the nuns were doing. She went into the kitchen where Sister Agnes was baking bread. "Good morning," she boomed. "Are you happy this morning, Sister Agnes?"

"Yes," she replied. "But I see you got up on the wrong side of the bed this morning, Mother."

The head of the convent was puzzled by the comment, but she moved on to the dairy, where Sister Margaret Mary was milking cows. "And how are you this fine day, Sister?" she asked.

"Fine," Margaret Mary replied. "But I see you got up on the wrong side of the bed."

"I did not," the Mother Superior insisted. She stormed into the laundry, where Sister Veronica was washing clothes. "Tell me," she began, "do you think I got up on the wrong side of the bed this morning?"

"Yes, I'm afraid I do," Sister Veronica said meekly.

"How can you tell?"

"Because you've got Father O'Brian's slippers on."

The nuns ran an orphanage in a rural area. One day the Mother Superior called in three teenage girls who were about to leave. "You're going out into a sinful world," she said. "I must warn you that men will take advantage of you. They'll buy you drinks and dinner, take you to their apartments, undress you, and do terrible things to you. Then they'll give you twenty or thirty dollars and kick you out."

"Excuse me, Mother," one of the teenagers said. "You mean men will take advantage of us and give us money?"

"Yes, child. Why do you ask?"

"Because the priests only give us candy."

The nuns were getting very restless in the August heat. The Mother Superior called a meeting to ask what was wrong.

One of the young novices said boldly, "What we need are some men around here."

The Mother Superior was shocked, but another nun added, "It's only human nature."

The Mother Superior thought for a moment, then said, "All right, I'll issue candles. You can comfort yourself with them."

"No, no," the nuns cried. "We've tried those."

The Reverend Mother was indignant. "They were good enough for me when I was young."

"Yes," said a nun, "but we get tired of the same thing, wick in and wick out."

The new bride wanted to make sure she was doing everything properly. She went to confession at church and asked the priest, "Is it alright to have intercourse just before Communion?"

"Of course, my dear," the priest replied. "As long as we don't make too much noise."

Who earns the most at the hospital—the doctor, the priest, or the rabbi?

The rabbi—he gets all the tips.

A young priest was startled to hear the confession of a very young girl who announced that her major sin was that she loved to suck cocks. At a loss for the proper penance for this vile, unnatural sin, the young priest excused himself for a moment and went back into the vestry and told the monsignor what he'd heard.

"That must be Jenny Riley," the monsignor said.

"So you've heard her confession," the young priest said. "What did you give her?"

"Ten dollars," the monsignor replied. "Though you can probably get away with five."

After spending a forbidden night on the town, two young nuns were trying to sneak back through the fence surrounding their convent. "You know," one giggled as she held the wire apart for the other to crawl through, "I feel like a Marine."

"So do I," the other said. "But where are we going to find one at this hour of the morning?"

God decided he needed a vacation. One of his aides suggested Venus. "Forget it," God said. "I went there 10,000 years ago and got sunburned."

Another aide suggested Jupiter. "No way," God replied. "I went there 5,000 years ago and froze my ass off."

A third advisor suggested Earth. "That's the worst," God answered angrily. "I was there 2,000 years ago, and they're still accusing me of knocking up some Jewish chick."

The Catholic cardinal was sitting with his aides, signing papers and proclamations. The phone rang, and a secretary answered.

"Your excellency," she said. "It's about the abortion bill. A reporter . . ."

"Don't bother me," the cardinal interrupted.

"But he wants to know what you're going to do about the bill."

"Just pay it," the cardinal replied. "Pay it quick."

The captain of the merchant ship was determined to stop his sailors from buggering each other during long voyages. He finally purchased some barrels and told the crew that there would be a bonus for every man if they filled the barrels with semen by the end of the voyage. Sure enough, the barrels were filled. To help pay the bonus, the captain decided to sell the semen to be made into wax.

The ship soon set sail for another voyage, and on the return the barrels were filled to the brim again. The captain called in the merchant about selling him another load, but he was surprised when the merchant called him a no-good son of a bitch.

"What's the matter?" the captain asked. "Didn't the load make good candles?"

"That it did," the merchant replied. "And I sold the batch to the convent. Now all of the nuns are pregnant!"

Chapter Six:

MORE FOUL HOMOSEXUAL JOKES

How can you tell a gay bar?

All the bar stools are turned upside down.

Did you hear about the really tough, butch dyke?

She walked into a locker room full of female wrestlers and offered to lick everyone in the place.

Is it better to be black or gay?

Black. You don't have to tell your mother.

What's the biggest crime committed by transvestites?

Male fraud.

Why does Santa Claus only have seven reindeer?

Because Prancer moved in with a hairdresser in Beverly Hills.

How many gays does it take to change a light bulb?

Three. One to call the lighting designer, one to serve hors d'oeuvres, and one to exclaim, "Oh, it's just fabulous!"

A cowboy unknowingly walked into a gay bar and announced, "I'm so thirsty, I could lick the sweat off a cow's balls."

From the back of the room came the cry, "Moo. Moo."

The eldest son of a respectable Boston family announced to his shocked father that he intended to live openly with his gay boyfriend.

"Damn it, Rodney," the father said. "Our family came over on the Mayflower, and we've never had a scandal like this."

"But Father, I love him."

"That doesn't matter. For God's sake, he's Catholic!"

To cut down on expenses, the two secretaries decided to vacation together and to share a hotel room. On the first night, one turned to her friend and rested her hand on her shoulder. "There's something about myself I've never told you," she admitted. "I'll be frank . . ."

"No," her friend interrupted, "I'll be Frank."

The very swishy man walked into Western Union and asked the operator, "Do you wire flowers?"

"Of course," she replied.

"Then send me to New York. I'm a pansy."

Did you hear about the interior decorator who was all black-and-blue after an auto accident?

He committed suicide because he clashed with his drapes.

Why did the homosexual get beaten up in the bar?

He walked in, stuck out his tongue, and asked the bartender to put a head on it.

The new inmate at the mental institution swore he was Napoleon. The head psychiatrist was particularly interested, because the institution had another long term patient who swore he, too, was Napoleon. The psychiatrist decided to put the two of them in the same room and see what happened. It was a calculated risk, because the men might react violently, but the chance of a cure was worth the gamble. And fortunately, the men spent the night without sounds of a disturbance.

The new patient was the first one up in the morning. The shrink hurried up to him and asked, "So now do you still think you're Napoleon?"

The man grinned coyly at him and said, "Of course not, silly. I'm the Empress Josephine."

Everybody was surprised when the extremely swishy Rodney announced his engagement to a young girl. A lot of skeptics made bets that he wouldn't go through with it, but they lost their money when the ceremony took place and Rodney actually took the girl on a honeymoon. Upon his return, he ran into a bunch of the losers in his favorite gay bar. "Well," one said sarcastically, "is that little bitch pregnant now?"

"God, I hope so," Rodney said with a grimace. "I don't think I could go through with that again."

A homosexual was walking down the street with a midget under his arm. He spotted a swishing friend and called out, "Hey, look what I found. You want to take a drag before I throw him out?"

The five-alarmer had been raging out of control for hours, pouring thick smoke over the street. At last the blaze was under control and the fire chief began accounting for his men. Two were missing, and he ordered a search.

Captain Kelly finally rounded a fire truck parked in an alley and found, to his shock, one fireman with his trousers down leaning over a garbage can and another fireman screwing him in the ass.

"What's the meaning of this?" the captain roared.

"Jones here had passed out from smoke inhalation," the fireman doing the fucking panted.

"You're supposed to give mouth to mouth resuscitation for that," the captain said.

"That's what started this," the fireman replied.

Bill joined the Foreign Legion, and was assigned to a fort way out in the Sahara Desert, far from any town. During his orientation session, he asked the sergeant what the Legionnaires did when they had to relieve their urge.

"The desert provides, son," the sergeant said. "When you feel the need at night, go to the hut by the pine tree outside the fort. There's a hole in the side. Stick your dick in the hole and you'll get relief."

Bill was very skeptical, but soon he was about to go out of his skull. He waited until the sun descended, then ran out to the hut and stuck his dick in the hole. Sure enough, a pair of warm lips surrounded his member and quickly brought him to ecstasy.

Bill suddenly had a new view of life in the Legion. He

visited the hut the next night, and the third. But on the fourth night, when he thrust his penis in, nothing happened. He rushed back, found the sergeant, and asked him what the hell was going on.

"Forgot to tell you," the sergeant said. "It's your night to sit in the hut."

How do they separate the men from the boys in San Francisco?

With a crowbar.

Did you hear about the two fags who had an argument in a gay bar?

They went outside to exchange blows.

What are the three things homosexuals like most?

To eat, drink, and be Mary.

One gay guy visited another in the hospital. "What did they do?" he asked the man lying in bed.

"They removed my tonsils, pulled out my teeth, and cut out my hemorrhoids."

"My God!" gasped the visitor. "A complete hysterectomy!"

What did the homosexual Apache want more than anything in the world?

A few bucks to eat on.

The young couple checked into what they thought was a quiet, respectable hotel. But when the man opened the drapes of his room, he looked out across an airshaft into a room a few feet away where three men were stacked like pancakes, butt-fucking the one in front of them.

Outraged, the man called for the manager, who came up to the room and looked out the window on the perverted scene. "Well," the guest said, "what do you make of that?"

The manager shook his head. "Lucky Ralph," he said. "He always gets to be the one in the middle."

What do rabbis do with foreskins after circumcisions?

They sell them to gays for chewing gum.

The homosexual finally got up the courage to tell his mother about his sexual preference. He went into the beauty salon where she worked as a manicurist and said, "Mom, I've got to talk with you."

"Sit down," she said, "I'll do your nails while we talk."

She went to work while the son started to bare his secret. "There's something I must tell you," he said. "It's bothered me for a couple of years. I don't know how to—"

"Is it that you're gay?" she suddenly interrupted.

"But how did you know?"

"It wasn't hard," his mother said. "You've got shit under your fingernails."

The wealthy homosexual checked into a country inn and was immediately captivated by the blond teenage bellboy. Late that night he rang for the boy and asked, "Do you like champagne?"

"Never had it, sir," the naive lad replied.

"Well, I love it, and I hate to drink alone," the fag said. "Bring two bottles and we'll share."

The bellboy complied, but midway through the second bottle he passed out. The homosexual immediately pulled down the boy's pants and had his way.

The next day the bellboy was moaning and groaning. "That champagne stuff is murder," he complained to a chambermaid.

"Bad headache, huh?" the chambermaid asked.

"The headache isn't so bad," the boy replied. "But champagne sure makes your asshole hurt like hell."

One fag told another that he'd picked up a gorgeous sailor the night before.

"Ooooh," the other moaned. "I wish I'd been there. I love sea food."

A week after they had split up, one fag came back to the apartment and said he'd forgotten to pack his paisley necktie.

"Oh, you can just kiss my ass," the other fag sneered.

"Listen, I didn't come to make up. I just want my necktie."

A fag went into a bar and met a big, burly truck driver, and they soon left together. The next day, the fag came back in, all battered, bruised, and bandaged. The bartender asked, "What happened?"

"Well," the fag replied, "that truck driver I left with wined and dined me, then took me up to his apartment. He gave me a bath, powdered me, and put me in a beautiful negligee. Then he picked me up in his arms, carried me over to the window by the moonlight, and asked me, 'Are you my little nightingale?'

"I said yes, and he replied, 'Well, fly, you fucker!', and he threw me out the window."

An American drinking in an English pub was amazed to see an Englishman sipping a Major Bailey—his favorite, a julep made with gin. They got to talking and discovered they had exactly the same taste in music, theater, books, sports, politics, and everything else. At last the pub keeper called, "Time, gentlemen."

The two had one last Major Bailey and left together. On the way out, the Englishman asked, "By the way, old chap, are you a homosexual?"

Startled, the American replied, "No. Are you?"

"I'm afraid not. Pity, isn't it?"

What do you call three lesbians in bed together?

Menage a twat.

Why did the gay philanthropist try to bribe the postal service to put his picture on a postage stamp?

So everybody in the country could lick his behind.

How can you tell a gay church service?

Only half the congregation is kneeling.

The convicted rapist was brought up in front of the state parole board for review. The chairman of the board looked over the man's record, which had dozens of arrests for unnatural sex acts with women. Then he asked the prisoner, "Can we really believe that this prison term has cured you of your perversions?"

"Oh, yes," the prisoner said. "Just ask the guard who's standing behind me. I'll never touch another woman again, will I, darling?"

Why did the homosexual suspect his live-in lover had been cheating on him?

Because he came home shit-faced.

What's the difference between a vulture and a male hairdresser?

A vulture won't eat a man until after he's dead.

Chapter Seven:

MORE LEWD SENIOR CITIZEN JOKES

The little old woman woke up in the middle of the night, reached down to pull up the covers, and felt her hand brush something hard on her husband's side of the bed. Squealing with joy, she jumped on board.

The old man woke up, bellowing, "Get off me, you fool woman, and call the doctor. I've got a strangulated hernia."

Two old men were discussing the recent demise of a friend. "You've got to admire Harry," one said. "He died for his beliefs."

"I didn't know he was a dedicated person," the other said. "What did he believe?"

"He believed he could live the life of a twenty-one-year-old with a seventy-one-year-old body."

After providing mediocre service to the wealthy widow, the young stud was distressed when she tried to pay him by check. He grudgingly accepted the payment, then complained, "Hey, this isn't a check. It's only a stub."

"That makes us even," the widow replied.

Two spinsters were walking into town when a man leaped out of the bushes. He pulled one to the ground and raped her. When it was over, the spinster asked her friend, "What are we going to do? How can I explain to the police I was raped twice in one night?"

"Twice?" asked her puzzled friend.

"Well, we are coming back this way, aren't we?"

Grandpa got drunk one night and no one could find him. They looked everywhere—behind the barn, in the hayshed—but no Grandpa. Finally, John heard the sows snorting and went to check. There was Grandpa, lying in the mud with an old sow and stroking her belly. "Gee, Grandma," John heard him mutter, "I been sleepin' with you for 49 years, and this is the first time I've noticed your nightgown has two rows of buttons."

An old maid was held up in a dark alley. She explained she had no money, but the robber insisted that it must be in her bra and started feeling around.

"I told you I haven't got any money," the spinster said. "But if you keep doing that, I'll write you a check."

"Send someone over quickly!" the old woman screamed into the phone. "Two naked bikers are climbing up toward my bedroom window."

"This is the Fire Department, lady," the voice replied. "I'll have to transfer you to the Police Department."

"No, it's you I want," she yelled. "They need a longer ladder."

The little boy told his mother he wanted to pee. "I'll take you to the bathroom," she replied.

"No," the boy said, "I want Grandma to take me."

"Why do you want Grandma instead of me?" the mother asked.

"Because her hand shakes."

Two octogenarians married and tottered off on their honeymoon. On their first night, they undressed and climbed into bed. A few moments later, the man turned toward his wife and slipped his hand into hers. On the following night, he again held her hand until they fell asleep. On the third night, the old bridegroom once again moved to take his bride's hand.

"Not tonight, dear," she said. "I have a headache."

A furious pounding in a hotel room late at night awakened a number of guests. The hotel detective was called, and he let himself into the room. Inside, he found an elderly man banging away on the wall with both fists as he cursed.

"Stop that," the detective said. "You're disturbing the whole hotel."

"Damn the hotel," the elderly man spat. "It's the first erection I've had in years, and both my hands are asleep."

A seventy-year-old man met a friend on the street and asked him what he'd been doing lately. The friend said he'd just spent six months in jail on a rape charge.

"Rape?" questioned the first man. "At your age? That's ridiculous."

"I know," replied the other. "But I was so flattered, I pleaded guilty."

The eighty-six-year-old tycoon married his twenty-two-year-old secretary. She waited nervously in bed until the man came out in his nightshirt. He went over to his bride and held up five fingers.

She said in a startled tone, "You want to do it five times?"

"No," he said. "I want you to pick a finger."

What's the definition of aging?

When you're not as good as you once were, but you're as good as you were *once*.

What's the height of precaution?

An old lady putting a condom on her candle.

An unhappy old woman confided to her niece, a recent bride, "Whatever you do, when you quarrel, resist the temptation to make cracks about your husband's love making."

"Why?" the young woman asked.

"I did that a few years ago," the old woman said sourly. "And in all the times since, I've never been able to get the thing straight between us again."

What's invisible and smells like dog food?

Old people's farts.

Chapter Eight:

MORE RAUNCHY SEX JOKES

Did you hear about the incredibly dumb hooker?

She came to New York to hustle and ended up in a warehouse.

How can you spot a serious artist?

He's the one who stays to paint a bowl of fruit after the nude model leaves.

What are the words a man least likes to hear?

"Only if you show me your vasectomy scar first."

A man was swimming in a crowded public pool when his bathing suit fell off. He swam around for a while, but couldn't find it. He stayed in a corner of the pool trying to think how he could get out of the water. Finally, he cupped one hand over his erect penis, jumped out of the water, and started for the locker room, yelling, "MAD DOG, MAD DOG!"

Everybody stopped in their tracks, stunned. Then a shapely girl jumped in front of the man, pulled down the bottom of half of her bikini, and shouted, "Let's muzzle the son of a bitch!"

The young girl confided to her girl friend, "The strangest thing has been happening to me. Every time I sneeze, I'm overtaken by an unbelievable sensation of wild passion."

"That's amazing," her friend said. "What do you take for it?"

The girl smiled. "Lots of black pepper."

Jenny, an aspiring young actress, made the rounds of producers' offices for months before finally landing a part in a police movie. The first day's shooting called for her to be thrown from a speeding car and tumble into a stack of garbage cans. On the second day, she was set on fire and thrown from a third floor window. On the third day, she was beat up by the villain and dumped into the sewage-laden river.

Wearily, she dragged herself from the water and limped to the production office. "Listen," she managed to stammer. "Who do I have to sleep with to get out of this movie?"

A sex researcher called one of the participants in a recent survey to check on a discrepancy. "In response to the question of frequency of intercourse," the researcher said, "you answered 'twice weekly.' Your wife, on the other hand, said 'several times per night.'"

"That's right," the man said. "But that's only until the second mortgage is paid off."

A man decided he had to kill his wife, so he asked his best friend, a doctor, for some poison. The doctor told him that any drug could be detected in an autopsy. Instead, he suggested the man go home and have intercourse with his wife eight times a day for three weeks.

Two weeks passed, and the doctor didn't hear a word, so he decided to drop in on his friend. When he arrived, he saw a shriveled up old man sitting in a rocking chair on the porch. Coming closer, he was shocked to see his friend, who looked like he'd aged twenty years.

Then, out of the front door, came the wife. She looked twenty years younger, and she flashed a smile at the doctor as she sauntered by in her bikini.

"My God, your wife looks great," the doctor said to his friend.

"Yeah," the friend whispered with a weak smile. "She doesn't even know she's about to die!"

The man and his secretary arrived very late at the hotel for the convention. The desk clerk told them that the hotel was booked up, and that only one room was available. They had no choice but to share the room.

They went upstairs, chastely dressed for bed in the bathroom, and retired on the separate twin beds. Shortly after the lights went out, the secretary called out, "Mr. Coffey, would you please close the window?"

The executive replied, "How would you like to be Mrs. Coffey for the night, my dear?"

"I'd love to," the young thing said.

"Good. Then you get up and close the damn window!"

How can you tell a female Hershey bar?

It's the one without the nuts.

Why did God create women?

He couldn't find a sheep that would do windows.

A woman walked into a bar carrying a duck. A drunk saw her and said, "Hey, what are you doing with that pig?"

The woman looked at him coldly and replied, "This isn't a pig. It's a duck."

"I know," the drunk said. "I was talking to the duck."

Two car salesmen were sitting at the bar. One complained to the other, "Boy, business sucks. If I don't sell more cars this month, I'm going to lose my fucking ass." Too late, he noticed a beautiful blonde sitting two stools away. Immediately, he apologized for his bad language.

"That's okay," the blonde replied. "If I don't sell more ass this month, I'm going to lose my fucking car."

An unfortunate young man broke his penis the day before his wedding. The doctor insisted that the injured member be placed in a plaster cast.

The next night, in the honeymoon suite, the young man lay in bed and watched in agony as his young wife came into the bedroom dressed in a transparent negligee. She cupped her huge breasts and said, "Look at these breasts, untouched by any man." Then she caressed her snatch, saying, "Look at this pussy, untouched by a man's hands." Then she lay on the bed and said, "Come on, honey, let's get to it."

Unable to stand his frustration, the man stood up, ripped off his shorts, and blurted, "Look at this prick, dear. Still in it's original wrapper."

A man was selling strawberries door-to-door. At one house a gorgeous young woman answered. She said she was interested, and told the man to go around to the back door. When he got to the rear of the house, he saw the woman standing in the door stark naked. Immediately, he started sobbing uncontrollably. Confused, the woman asked him what was wrong.

The man replied, "Last month I lost my job. Last week my wife left me, and yesterday my house burned down. Now I'm going to get fucked out of my strawberries."

An eighteen-year-old boy was drinking in a bar. He asked an older man sitting next to him, "I want to learn all about women. What do you call that little magic button in a woman's slit?"

"A clitoris."

"What's the brown part around the nipples?"

The older man replied, "That's the areola."

"Wow, you know everything," the boy said. "How about that smooth patch of skin between a woman's cunt and her asshole?"

The older man thought for a moment, then answered, "I don't recall the scientific name. But most of the fellas around here call it a chin rest."

What's a clitoris?

A female hood ornament.

At a rape trial, the young victim was asked by the D.A. what the defendant said before the alleged assault. Too embarrassed to answer aloud, the victim asked if she could write out the answer. After reading the note, the judge instructed it to be passed along to the jurors.

One juror, who had dozed off, was nudged by the woman juror next to him. He took the note from her and read, "I'm going to fuck you like you've never been fucked before." The juror smiled to the woman and slipped the note in his pocket.

"Will juror number 12 please pass the note to me!" ordered the judge.

"I can't, your honor," he said. "It's too personal."

While away at a convention, an executive happened to meet a young woman who was pretty, chic, and intelligent. When he persuaded her to disrobe in his hotel room, he found out she had a superb body as well. Unfortunately, the executive found himself unable to perform.

On his first night home, the executive padded naked from the shower into the bedroom to find his wife swathed in a rumpled bathrobe, her hair curled, her face creamed, munching candy loudly while she pored through a movie magazine. And then, without warning, he felt the onset of a magnificent erection.

Looking down at his throbbing member, he snarled, "Why you ungrateful, mixed-up son of a bitch. Now I know why they call you a prick!"

When the teenagers' petting session had reached a certain point, the girl suddenly disengaged herself, unzipped her date, and performed oral sex. When it was over, she whispered, "Eddie, did you like it?"

"I sure did," he replied. "But Nancy, I had no idea you were queer."

When Adam noticed that the animals were going off into the woods together and emerging looking contented, he asked Eve about it. "You idiot," she said. "That's reproduction."

"Lord," Adam asked the next time God came around, "what's reproduction?"

"Experience is the best teacher," the Lord replied. "Why don't you go into the woods with Eve and find out."

Adam followed the advice. A little later he came back out to God and asked, "Lord, what's a headache?"

A couple slept in separate bedrooms, and the man was awakened one night by his wife's screams. He rushed into her room and snapped on the light just in time to see a male figure flee through the window. "That man attacked me twice!" the wife screamed.

"Then why didn't you yell sooner?" the husband asked.

"Because I thought it was you," the wife replied. "Until he began to start on the second time."

What's male pubic hair?

A dick Vandyke.

What's masturbation?

A self-service elevator.

What's the ultimate in singles bars?

One where the girls have to show their I.U.D.s to get in.

What's the best defense against rape?

Beat off the attacker.

Did you hear about the sperm bank that is going to sell its product in aerosol containers?

It's called Heirspray.

What company is the leading manufacturer of vibrators?

Genital Electric.

What do you get when you mix marijuana with an aphrodisiac?

Tumbleweed.

"Grrr," said the wolf, leaping at Little Red Riding-hood. "I'm going to eat you."

"Shit," the girl replied. "Doesn't anybody fuck anymore?"

While swimming nude, the college student got a terrible sunburn all over his body. Later that night, alone in bed with his date, he found the agony unbearable. Stepping into the kitchen, he poured a glass of cold milk and submerged his penis in it.

"My God!" the girl gasped, watching in the doorway. "I've always wondered how men load that thing."

On the morning after their wedding night, the groom called room service to order breakfast. He requested bacon and eggs for himself, and a plate of lettuce for his bride. "Would the lady care for anything else?" the puzzled clerk asked.

"Not right now," the groom replied. "I just want to see if she eats like a rabbit, too."

"You're going to find this hard to believe," the beautiful young girl told her doctor, "but I've been married three times, and I'm still a virgin."

"How can that be possible?" he asked.

"Well, my first husband was a psychiatrist, and he only talked about it. The second was a gynecologist, and he only looked at it. And the third was a gourmet."

A man waiting outside the delivery room had been really obnoxious to the nurses. When his wife finally gave birth, they decided to shake him up by bringing out a black baby to show him.

"Well," one nurse said, waiting for a reaction, "what do you think?"

"Cute kid," the man said.

"Don't you think it's strange that the baby is black?"

"Nah," the man said, "my fucking wife burns everything."

An old fashioned gentleman took a very modern girl out for a date. When they got back to her apartment, they started to kiss. The gentleman said, "This is called spooning. Do you like it?"

"It's okay," she replied. "But I'd rather shovel."

While visiting the U.S., a French girl ran out of money just before her visa expired. She was in despair until she ran into a sailor who told her he'd smuggle her aboard his ship and bring her food during the voyage. All she'd have to do in return is provide sexual services. Desperate, the girl agreed.

Late that night, the sailor sneaked her on board the vessel, and twice each day afterwards brought her food and received his reward. Finally, after nearly two weeks, the captain became suspicious and followed the sailor. He witnessed the rather original bartering, then confronted the girl.

She told him the whole story. He looked at her a moment, then said, "Hmmm, rather clever of that young seaman. However, miss, I feel it's only fair to tell you that this isn't an ocean liner—it's the Staten Island Ferry."

The very proper Bostonian young lady finally found a suitably blue-blooded young man to marry. After a lavish wedding, the bride and groom found themselves naked in their hotel room.

"Are you sure you're ready for this, my dear?" the considerate groom asked.

"Yes," the bride said resolutely. "Mother had a talk with me. I will do my duty."

The groom set to work. Being more than a little experienced, he soon had his wife writhing with passion. Just as they neared the climax of the act, the young lady moaned, "Oh, darling. Is this what the servants call fucking?"

"Yes, my dear."

"Ah," the girl moaned. "We've got to stop that. It's much too good for them."

"Ho, ho, ho!" Santa exclaimed as he slid down the chimney. When he arrived at the bottom, he found a statuesque nude brunette waiting for him. "Merry Christmas, Santa," the woman said seductively. "I'm your present."

"Sorry," Santa said. "But it's my busy night. I've got to go."

He went back up the chimney, flew to the next roof, then slid down. At the bottom, he found a voluptuous blonde, who gleefully offered herself to the jolly old man.

"Can't do it," Santa said with regret. "Millions of children are waiting for their toys." And off he went.

A few moments later, he entered a third house. This time he saw a beautiful redhead spread out on the floor.

Santa had always been partial to redheads, and this woman had the biggest tits he'd ever seen. Despite his time schedule, he was sorely tempted.

"Come on, Santa," the woman said seductively, "I'm going to knock those red socks of yours off."

"Might as well," Santa said, looking down at the swelling that was bulging the seams of his pants. "I can't get up the chimney now anyway."

During World War II, the Fuhrer issued orders that his elite SS troops were to rape as many women as possible in captured cities and towns. After the rape, the SS soldier was ordered to stand, give the Nazi salute, and announce, "In nine months you will have a baby. Name it Adolf Hitler."

One SS soldier stationed in France didn't have the heart for rape. Finally, however, the jeering of his comrades was so hard to take that he went out determined to take advantage of the first girl he met. Outside a village, he saw a frail, weak-looking girl and he fell upon her. After the rape, he stood, clicked his heels, shot his right arm in the air, and said, "In nine months you shall have a baby. Name it Adolph. Heil Hitler."

She replied, "In three days, you will have a disease. Name it syphilis. Vive la France!"

Harvey was standing in front of the urinal in the men's locker room when Calvin, the black assistant golf pro, came up next to him. Harvey couldn't resist taking a peek.

"Hey," Harvey said. "It's true. You black guys really are hung."

"It isn't only being black," Calvin replied. "We do exercises for it."

"What kind?"

"Well, for one thing, we slap our pricks five times every night before we get into bed."

Harvey decided to try it. His wife was already in bed when he got home. He undressed in the bathroom, crept in, then slapped his penis five times. He was crawling between the covers when his wife called out, "Calvin, is that you?"

After his first wife died, the boss married his gorgeous young secretary. Soon, however, she was tired of being left alone on weekends, so she decided to take up golf. She arranged for a series of lessons with the young pro.

He put a club in her hands on the first lesson and told her to swing. "Not bad," he said. "I think you might be a natural. But you've got to hold the club gently."

"How gently?" she asked.

"Well," he said. "Say, hold the club as if it were your husband's penis."

The woman complied. "Much better," the pro said after a couple swings. "Now if you take the club out of your mouth, you'll be fine."

The old drunk found a $10 bill lying on the sidewalk, and he decided that he'd use the unexpected fortune to buy himself the kind of time he hadn't had in years. After downing his pint, he staggered into a whorehouse and demanded a girl from the madam.

She was about to kick him out, but then she realized that the guy was so far in the bag he wouldn't know what the hell he was doing. So she took the ten bucks and escorted him up to a room in which reclined a life-size inflatable doll. Sure enough, the old drunk let out a whoop, dropped his pants, and hopped on.

The madam went downstairs. But a few moments later, a horrible howl of agony came from the room. The madam rushed back up to find the old man weeping bitterly.

"What happened? Didn't you have a good time?" the madam asked.

"We had a great time," the drunk said through his tears. "Then I bit her on the ass, she let out a huge fart and flew out the window!"

The young girl was just off the boat from France. Soon many young men were competing for her. One handsome bachelor had an edge on the rest and was able to convince her to go for a drive on lovers' lane.

They sat in the car necking for a while, then the French girl said she needed a breath of fresh air. She got out of the car, took a few steps, then let out a huge shriek.

The young man rushed to her side as the girl pointed to a used condom lying on the ground. "That's all right," the young man said. "Don't they use those things in France?"

"*Mais, oui,*" the young girl said. "But we don't skin them!"

George arrived home incredibly horny after a week long business trip. His wife, however, was in a terrible mood. They ended up in a violent argument, and George stormed out of the apartment and down the stairs. As he opened the front door, however, he ran into the woman downstairs, who asked him what was wrong. He told her, she invited him in to talk about it, and one thing led to another until they were rolling in bed.

A couple of hours later, he staggered back upstairs. His wife started to continue the argument, but he cut her off, saying, "Listen, you could learn a few things from Jean downstairs. She knows how to treat a man. I was so happy after we climbed out of the sack that I gave her $25."

"Oh, yeah," his wife retorted. "Her husband gives me $50."

The barber had finished cutting the hair of an obnoxious customer. He opened a bottle of cologne and was about to splash some on his customer when the man barked, "I don't want any of that crap. My wife will think I smell like a whorehouse."

The barber smiled. "I use this all the time. I'm lucky—my wife doesn't know what a whorehouse smells like."

The bank robbers herded the customers and tellers behind the counter and ordered them to take off all their clothes and lie face down on the floor.

One nervous female teller pulled off her dress and sprawled out, facing upwards.

"Turn over, Marilyn," hissed her girl friend. "This is a stick-up, not the office party."

Did you hear about the town nymphomaniac?

She was so thin that every time she swallowed an olive, four guys left town.

A man tried everything he could to attract the attention of a beautiful young girl sitting at the bar, but she continued to ignore him. Frustrated, he went up to her and sneered, "Pardon me, I thought you were my mother."

"I couldn't be," she replied cooly. "I'm married."

The show girls had entertained the troops all afternoon at a remote army base. After the performance, the major asked, "Would you girls like to mess with the enlisted men or the officers?"

"It doesn't matter," one bold girl replied. "But we would like something to eat first."

What's the definition of a perfect secretary?

One who takes dictation on both knees.

The three sisters got married on the same day. They decided to save money by spending the first night in their own house. Their mother stayed up all night listening in case any of the girls had any problems. All she heard was some laughing from her first daughter and some crying from the second. The third daughter was silent.

The next morning, the mother questioned the girls about what had happened. "You always told me to laugh when I was tickled," the first girl said.

"You always told me to cry when something hurt," the second said.

"You taught me never to talk with my mouth full," said the third.

Why did the young nymphomaniac fail her driving test?

Every time the car stopped, she jumped into the back seat.

A guy walked into a whorehouse one day, but all the girls laughed at him because he had "Shorty" tattooed on his dick. He walked from girl to girl and each one burst out laughing, until he got to the 25th whore. She took pity on him and took him upstairs.

An hour later she came down looking like she'd been run over by a truck. The other girls asked what happened. She replied, "Remember that guy with 'Shorty' tattooed on his dick? Well, when I got him hard, it said, 'Shorty's Bar and Grill, Albuquerque, New Mexico!'"

A bald man bought a hairpiece, hoping to improve his sex life. On his first date, he found himself back in his apartment, making it hot and heavy. Suddenly, he realized his hairpiece had fallen off. Groping in the dark to locate it before his date realized what happened, he inadvertently stuck his hand up his date's dress.

"That's it," she sighed.

"Oh, no," he replied. "I part mine on the side."

A young man was in love and wanted to propose, but he was ashamed of his tiny penis. After refusing to let her see him naked for a long time, he decided to bring up the matter subtly. He drove up to lovers' lane one night. In the darkness, he unzipped his pants and placed her hand on his organ.

"Thanks," she said. "But you know I don't smoke."

Two boys overheard two men walking out of a whorehouse talking about what they'd got for $20. One boy said, "I've got a dollar. Let's go in and see what we can get."

The madam answered the door and the boy told her he wanted a dollar's worth of what they were selling. The woman took the dollar, put her hand up her dress, rubbed her crotch, then rubbed it in the boy's face.

The boy turned to his friend and said, "If that's what you get for a dollar, I don't know how they can stand $20 worth."

What's the difference between a prostitute, a mistress and a wife?

A prostitute says, "Aren't you done yet?" A mistress asks, "Are you done already?" A wife comments, "I think the ceiling needs painting."

A cowboy was out riding on the range one day when he spotted a snake. He was about to shoot when the reptile said, "Hold it. I'm a magic snake. I'll give you three wishes if you'll spare me."

The cowboy eagerly agreed. "Okay. I want to be rich, handsome, and hung like my horse."

"Done," the snake said.

When the cowboy got back to the house, he was told the owner had died and left him the ranch. He looked in the mirror, and found he was incredibly good looking. But then he undid his trousers, and he screamed in agony, "My God! I forgot I was riding the gelding!"

A farm boy returned from the city and told his father, "Pop, I'm going to move to the city and plant a whole acre of hair."

"Hair? Why hair?"

"Because a city girl said she'd made $10,000 off a patch no bigger than the palm of your hand."

A man came home from work with two black eyes. "What happened?" his wife asked suspiciously.

"Well," he started, "I was sitting on the bus and this lady was standing in front of me. I noticed her dress was sticking in her crack and I politely pulled it out. She turned around and slugged me."

"How did you get the other black eye?" the wife demanded.

"Well, I figured she liked it the first way, so I put it back in."

After a six month affair, a young woman called her boyfriend and announced she was pregnant.

"That's the way it goes," he said. "Consider that a parting gift."

"Well, I also got back the results of my blood test," she said. "Why don't we consider it an even trade?"

A man suddenly found himself impotent and hurried to the doctor. The doctor gave him a potion to take, and warned him he mustn't miss a meal.

The following night, the patient was invited to a banquet. Not wanting to answer questions about the medicine, he privately instructed the waiter to place the dosage in his soup.

The other guests were all served their soup and were well on the way to finishing their meals when the impatient medicine taker asked to see the waiter.

"Where's my soup?" he demanded.

"I put in the medicine, sir," the waiter said. "Now I'm waiting for the noodles to lie down."

A guy walks into the local bar, looks around, and notices a good-looking girl at the other end. He walks over to her, sits down, takes a frog out of his pocket, puts it on the bar, and orders a drink.

She looks at the frog, then turns to him and asks, "What's the frog for?"

"That's my trained pet."

"What does he do?"

"He eats pussy," the man replied. She stands up, slaps him, and walks out of the bar.

Halfway down the street, however, her curiosity gets the better of her. She returns to the bar and after a few drinks asks the man for proof.

They go back to his apartment. He tells her to take off her clothes and lie on her back. He places the frog between her legs, but nothing happens.

"What's the story?" she asks the guy. "Why doesn't

he do something?"

The guy picks up the frog and puts him on the side of the bed. He starts to crawl between the girl's legs, saying, "Okay, frog, I'm going to show you for the last time."

Two women were talking about their early sex lives. "When I was 12," one said, "my brother used to screw me twice a week. My cunt was so tight he needed a shoehorn to get in."

"That's nothing," said the other. "When I was nine, my Dad used to put chocolate on his tool and say, 'Want some fudge?' To this day, I can't eat fudge unless it has nuts on it."

What do you get when you cross a rooster and a lollipop?

A cocksucker.

The man walked into the talent agent one day and opened a suitcase. Out popped a tiny man, who sat down at a miniature grand piano and played a brilliant solo.

"Amazing," the agent said. "Where did you get him?"

"Well," the man said, "I was walking through the fields in Ireland one day and I spotted a leprechaun, who told me I was granted one wish."

"And this was your wish?"

"Not exactly," the man said. "The leprechaun was hard of hearing. So I ended up with a 12-inch pianist."

A couple appeared before a judge in a divorce proceeding. "What's the grounds?" the judge asked.

"Cruel and inhumane punishment," the woman said. "He tied me to the bed, then forced me to sing the national anthem while he peed on me."

"That's horrible," the judge said.

"Yeah," the woman replied. "He knows how much I hate to sing."

Three truckers' wives were discussing the funny things their husbands did when they got home. The first said she woke up one night to find her husband pressing her belly button as if it were a starter.

"That's nothing," said the second. "I woke up one night with my husband straddling my body, squeezing my tits, and hollering at me to turn right."

"Well," said a third, "I'll tell you what my husband did. I woke up and he had my legs spread apart while mumbling to himself, 'Christ, how am I ever going to fix that flat.'"

The mother walked into the bathroom to find her son vigorously scrubbing his penis with a toothbrush and lots of toothpaste. "What are you doing?" she asked.

"Don't try to stop me," the boy warned. "I'm going to do this three times a day. I'm not going to get a cavity that smells as bad as my sister's does."

Did you hear about the hooker who used to be a real estate broker?

She charges by the pubic inch.

A businessman who had been away for several weeks went to a whorehouse and asked the madam for the lousiest lay in the place.

The madam looked at the man's very expensive suit and watch, and commented that he appeared to be a man who deserved the best.

"I want the lousiest lay," the man repeated. "I'm not horny, I'm homesick."

The young boy was beating off behind the house when he ejaculated into his hand. He looked at the semen and said, "You could have been a baseball player . . . a movie star . . . a famous lawyer . . . maybe even president."

He debated for a moment, then licked the cum off his hand, saying, "Okay, I'll give you another chance."

What are the two most useless things in the world?

A man's tits and the Pope's balls.

Why is a woman like a bank?

Because you lose interest when you withdraw your assets.

Did you hear about the man who constantly had cunt on the brain?

Every month he'd get a nosebleed.

The night before the wedding, the young girl came to her mother in tears. "I'm not so sure I can perform my wifely duties," the girl sobbed.

The mother put her arm around the girl and started gently explaining the facts of life. The girl interrupted her. "Mother," she said, "I'm not worried about that—I can fuck and suck with the best of them. But I can't cook."

The hotel supervisor found the pretty maid sitting in the locker room, obviously upset with herself. "What happened?" the supervisor asked.

"Well, there was a call from Room 403. When I got up there, this handsome man grabbed me, tore off my clothes, threw me on the bed, fucked me, then pushed me out the door."

"That's awful!" the supervisor exclaimed.

"Yeah," the maid said. "I never found out what he called for."

Two young actresses were talking in the studio cafeteria when one confided to the other that she'd been troubled by crabs. "Didn't they give you a powder to use?" the other asked.

"Yes."

"Didn't it kill the crabs?"

"Yeah," the first actress acknowledged. "But it also knocked out two producers and an agent."

A guy was boasting in a bar that he had a wonderful sense of smell. Other drinkers decided to put his powers to the test. The man was blindfolded, and a flower was held under his nose. "Daisy," the man replied confidently.

"Correct."

Another man had a twig from a tree. It only took the man with the sense of smell an instant to say, "Birch." The man made two more correct guesses before the bartender called the barmaid over, ran his middle finger under her skirt, and held it under the man's nose. "What's this?" the bartender asked.

"Fish," the man replied.

A small boy walked into a drugstore and asked the clerk for some condoms. "What size and who are they for?" the clerk asked.

"Give me assorted sizes," the kid said. "They're for my sister. She's going to the country."

A man walked into the drug store to buy some condoms. He didn't know the right size, so the lady proprietor invited him to the rear of the store for a measurement. She took his penis in one hand while she attempted to measure it. "Size 3, Mimi," she called out to her partner. "No, 4 . . . no, no . . . 7 . . . Mimi, it's an 8 . . . my God, Mimi, bring the mop!"

Two cops were patrolling the park when they heard a series of anguished moans coming from the bushes. They investigated and found a well-dressed but obviously very drunk businessman rolling on the ground with his hand over his groin.

"What's wrong?" one cop asked.

"God damn, my fucking prick," the drunk hissed through clenched teeth. "I met thish, thish hooker. I paid her $25 dollars to come into the park with me."

"And she kneed you in the balls?" the other cop asked.

"No," the man stammered. "She licked me and sucked me but my fucking prick wouldn't get hard."

"So?"

"So now I'm getting even with the little bastard. He's wanted to piss for the last hour, but I won't let him."

The bartender approached the dazed man sitting at the bar and asked, "Is anything the matter? You've been belting them down hard for hours."

"My wife died yesterday," the man replied.

"I'm sorry," the bartender said. "It must be hard to lose a wife."

"Hard!" the man laughed. "It was fucking near impossible."

A very homely young woman made an appointment with a psychiatrist. She walked into his office and said, "Doctor, I'm so depressed and lonely. I don't have any friends, no man will touch me, and everybody laughs at me. Can you help me accept my ugliness?"

"I'm sure I can," the psychiatrist replied. "Just go over and lie face down on that couch."

A couple told a marriage counselor that they still loved each other, but after ten years of marriage they didn't feel sexually excited.

"Build on the positive," the counselor advised. "If you both observe yourselves carefully, you'll find brief moments when you feel excited about each other. Write them down, and we'll talk about it next week."

At the next session, they told the counselor they only had one moment when sex crossed their minds—when they were eating lunch at McDonald's.

"Good," the counselor said. "Next time when you feel the urge at McDonald's, act on it."

Another week passed. The couple reported that they'd gone to McDonald's again, then they did it.

"How did it go?"

"Perfect," the couple replied. "But there's one trouble. We can't ever go back to McDonald's again."

A man started talking to a beautiful girl at a party. "Would you like a drink?" he asked.

She said she didn't drink.

"Would you like to go back to my place and screw?"

She said that she didn't do that either.

Exasperated, he said, "Then how about a bale of hay?"

"You're crazy," she said. "I don't eat hay."

"Just as I thought," the man replied. "You're not fit company for man or beast."

Why do women rub their eyes when they wake up in the morning?

Because they don't have balls to scratch.

What's the definition of a Peeping Tom?

A window fan.

A couple who were deeply into the psychic arts vowed that if one of them died, the other would try to make contact on the anniversary of the death. The husband died first, and a year later his wife and a group of friends sat around a table, joined hands, and began to chant the husband's name.

To their surprise, a voice called out, "Is that you, honey?"

"Oh, darling," the widow cried. "I can't believe it's you."

The husband started to ask about his wife's life and their friends, but she interrupted, saying, "I want to know about you. What do you do all day?"

He replied, "Well I get up in the morning and have sex, rest a while, have more sex, then I have lunch, then have sex again before dinner."

"My God," the women exclaimed. "Is that what heaven's like?"

"Hell, I'm not in heaven," the man said. "I've been reincarnated. I'm a jackrabbit in Arizona."

At a convention, a salesman met a stylish-looking woman at the bar, bought her a drink, and ended up going to her room for a long lovemaking session. But afterwards, as they lay in bed smoking, the salesman was suddenly filled with remorse. "I don't know what came over me," he said. "I'm happily married with a beautiful wife and four great kids. I'm so ashamed of myself."

The woman said soothingly, "Don't be so hard on yourself. People do a lot worse things than what you did. Take me for example. I knew I had herpes when I met you."

What's the definition of a chatter box?

A pussy with a vibrator inside.

What's a nymphomaniac's dilemma?

A guy with a ten-inch prick and herpes.

The woman was testifying in court how a man raped her standing in an alley.

"But," the judge said, "this man is much shorter than you are. How could he have raped you?"

"Well," the girl said a bit sheepishly, "I had to stoop a bit."

What's yellow and lays in a tree?

Tweety the whore.

The hooker sauntered into the corner liquor store to buy a bottle with the $20 bill a john had just given her. The owner took one look at the bill and handed it back, saying, "This bill is counterfeit. Somebody's fucked you."

"Fucked, hell," the hooker angrily replied. "I've been raped!"

What is the sexual position, "68?"

You do me and I'll owe you.

Why do women have legs?

So they don't leave snail trails when they walk.

A carpenter put up a partition in a whore house and asked the madam for $100 for the job. She replied that she didn't have $100 in cash, but the carpenter could take it out in trade. He asked if he could take it out on her, and she agreed.

She got undressed and lay on the bed. He stuck his thumb up her cunt and his index finger up her ass-hole, and said, "Give me the $100 now, or I pull out the partition."

A young maid was dusting a statue of a nude male when she accidently knocked it over, breaking off the penis. She quickly glued it back on, but when her employer's wife returned, she immediately noticed that the penis was sticking up in the air instead of hanging down. "You've got it wrong," the lady of the house told the maid.

"But madam," the maid said, "that's the only way I've ever seen them!"

Two disgusted men were sitting at a bar having a discussion about their wives. "What do you mean," asked one, "when you say you have to think twice before you leave your wife alone at night?"

"First," the other said, "I have to think up a reason for going out. And second, I have to think up a reason she can't go with me."

A couple was planning to drive to the seacoast for their vacation. The wife sent her husband to the drugstore to get her some Dramamine. The husband went on the errand, and while he was there he picked up some condoms, too.

The next day, the wife suggested that while they were at the coast, they ought to take an extra week and take a cruise. The husband agreed, and went back to the drugstore to get more supplies.

The druggist filled the order for condoms and Dramamine. As he handed the bag to the man he said, "Listen, buddy. I got to ask you a question. If fucking makes you that sick, why don't you just jerk off?"

What's the definition of a hyper-active hooker?

One who turns tricks so fast she has to hand out air-sickness bags.

A man picked up a woman in a bar and took her home. He got her clothes off, but before he could get his cock inside she told him that she'd been to the doctor that day and had been told that she either had VD or TB. She didn't remember which.

The man was so horny that he decided to call the woman's doctor. Pleading a life and death emergency, he finally got through to the doctor at home. Unfortunately, the doctor said he had so many patients that he couldn't remember what the woman had.

"But I got to know if it's VD or TB, Doc," the man begged.

"Listen," the doctor said. "I have a suggestion. Why don't you chase her around the room a few times. If she coughs, fuck her."

A New York City book salesman, traveling through the South, asked a village bookstore owner, "Have you seen our new book, 'Solving the Problem of Incest'?"

"That's what I hate about you Yankees," the Southerner sneered. "You take a nice family game and turn it into some goddamn problem."

The man was sitting in a bar when his buddy came in. The buddy ordered a drink, then turned and asked, "How you doing, Ed? Still getting some pussy on the side?"

The man grunted, then replied, "I haven't had any in so long that I didn't know they moved it."

Chapter Nine:

UTTERLY DISGUSTING

Why did Helen Keller have pockmarks all over her face?

From learning to eat with a fork.

Did you hear about the man who got arrested at the carnival?

He saw a man having an epileptic fit and he thought it was a new ride, so he jumped on.

What kind of vibrators do female elephants use?

Epileptics.

The traveling salesman approached an old farmhouse and noticed the strange behavior of the couple inside. The woman was running the lawnmower over the carpet and the man had one hand dipped in a fishbowl and was playing with himself with the other. The salesman assumed they were crazy and moved on.

After he'd finished his pitch at the next farmhouse, he mentioned what he'd just seen. "Oh, those folks ain't crazy," the farmer said. "They're both deaf mutes. She was telling him to mow the lawn, and he was telling her to go fuck herself because he was going fishing."

What's the hardest part about eating a vegetable?

The wheelchair.

What do you call the costume of a one-legged ballerina?

A one-one.

What did Helen Keller say when she passed the fish market?

Good afternoon, ladies.

Why was Helen Keller arrested on a morals charge?

For lip reading in the girls' locker room.

A woman told her husband that for her birthday, she wanted to take a champagne bath. Reluctantly, her husband agreed. He purchased a case of the bubbly and poured the contents of each bottle into the bathtub.

The woman hopped in and enjoyed herself immensely. Afterwards, her husband decided all that champagne shouldn't go to waste, so he began pouring it back into the bottles. When he was finished, he found he had a cup left over. "Oh, no, honey!" he cried in dismay. "You didn't!"

A woman got on an elevator at the first floor. Being the only one on the car, she decided to let out a horrendous fart. Then, to cover the smell, she sprayed some pine freshener.

At the sixth floor, an elderly gentleman got on and noticed the stench. The woman innocently asked him, "Isn't the smell in this elevator awful?"

"Yeah," the man replied. "It smells like someone shit in a pine tree."

The businessman took the young secretary to a motel room. The girl seemed shy and inexperienced, so the man decided he would be her tutor in the arts of love. He began by running his hands over her chest. "Do you know what I'm doing?" he asked.

"No," she replied.

"I'm fondling your breasts."

Then he moved his hand down to the soft V between her legs and asked, "Do you know what I'm doing now?"

When she replied, "No," he explained he was caressing her clitoris. Then he became so aroused that he spread her legs and thrust his penis into her.

"Do you know what I'm doing now?" he panted.

"Yes," she responded coolly. "You're catching herpes."

A man was sitting in a porno movie theater when suddenly he smelled an awful stench. He noticed a drunk was sitting a couple seats away, and he knew what the odor was.

"Hey," the man called, "did you shit in your pants?"

"Yeah," the drunk replied.

"Well, what are you going to do about it?" the man demanded.

"Don't know," the drunk said. "I haven't finished yet."

The incredibly horny man walked into the whorehouse with ten dollars. The only woman he could buy at that price was named Sandpaper Sally. The man took her upstairs, but after a few thrusts, he pulled out his sore cock and said, "Now I know how you got your name. It's damn rough in there."

"I'll fix that," Sally said, heading into the bathroom.

When she returned, the man resumed having sex. "Ah, that's better. What did you do?"

"Nothing much," she replied. "Just picked the scabs and let the pus run."

Two cannibals captured a missionary and decided to have him for lunch. One started eating at the head, the other at the feet. After a while, the one at the head asked the other how he liked the meal.

"Fine," the man replied. "I'm having a ball."

"Then slow down," said the first. "You're eating too fast."

A girl was coming home from a date. Her mother had waited up for her, and when the girl walked in the door, the mother noticed she had rice in her hair. "Anne," she said, "you didn't tell me you were going to a wedding."

"I didn't, Mother," Anne replied. "I was blowing a Chinaman and he got sick all over me."

Fred was standing at the bar when the stripper came onstage. As she began to dance, the man behind him screamed in his ear, "Take it off!" Fred turned around to glare, and the man apologized. A few minutes later, the dancer peeled off her dress, and once again the man bellowed in Fred's ear, "Take it off!" Fred turned around and told him to lay off or he'd call the manager, and once again the man apologized. But the man screamed even louder when the stripper peeled off her bra and her panties, and Fred was furious.

Finally, the dancer took off her G-string and the crowd went wild. It was a moment before Fred realized the man behind him was quiet. He turned around and said, "Where's your enthusiasm now, buddy?"

"All over your back, pal," the man said.

What's the difference between a bartender and a proctologist?

A proctologist only has to deal with one asshole at a time.

A hard-to-please lady was in the bedding department of a large department store. She bent over to feel a mattress and inadvertently let out a fart. Blushing and hastily straightening up, she begged the pardon of the salesman standing behind her.

"That's okay, lady," the salesman replied. "When you hear the price of that mattress, you're going to shit."

A man who smoked a dozen cigars a day tried everything to give up the habit. Finally, he visited a doctor, who promised him a foolproof method. "You're going to think this is unusual," the doctor said. "But every night before you go to bed, I want you to insert a cigar all the way into your rectum. The next morning, pull it out, put it back in the wrapper, then place it with the rest of your stogies. That way you can't tell which one you've treated and you won't smoke any of them."

The man was skeptical, but he decided to try it. A month later, he went back to the doctor and reported he'd been able to break the habit.

"Great," the doctor said. "I'm happy to hear of your success."

"Yeah, but I've developed another problem."

"What's that?" the doctor asked.

The man replied, "Now I can't get to sleep without sticking a cigar up my ass."

A man found a magic lamp. He rubbed it and a genie appeared. The genie offered him one wish.

"I want to be rock hard and get plenty of ass for the rest of my life," the man said.

So the genie turned him into a commode.

What's the definition of constipation?

A log jam.

A man sat at the bedside of his dying wife. Her voice was little more than a whisper.

"Darling," she said, "I have a confession to make. I'm the one who took $25,000 from your safe. I spent it on a fling with your best friend. I was the one who paid your mistress to leave town. And I reported your income tax evasion to the I.R.S. Can you ever forgive me?"

"Of course, dear," the man said. "I'm the one who poisoned you."

An Arab, lost in the desert and feeling the end was near, decided to have sex with his favorite camel. But he was so weak he couldn't manage to hold the animal down. They continued to wander aimlessly around until they neared a tiny oasis. A woman ran out, shouting a greeting.

"What . . . what are you doing here?" asked the surprised Arab.

"My wicked stepfather abandoned me when I would not let him have his way with me," the girl said as she unveiled herself to reveal her considerable charms. "But you have rescued me, and I will do anything you want, right here and now."

"Wonderful," the Arab cried. "Hold down this camel."

A farm boy, intrigued by the possibilities of the automatic milking machine, decided to try it on himself. After a highly satisfactory cycle had been completed, though, he tried without success to work the nozzle off. He called for his father, who called the salesman. "What should I do?" the father asked. "My boy can't get his doohickey loose."

"You'd better call down to the fish store for some oysters," the salesman replied. "That there machine is set for four quarts."

On an isolated stretch of beach near Cannes, a beautiful French girl threw herself into the sea and drowned in despair, despite a young passerby's attempts to save her. The man dragged the half-nude body ashore and left it on the sand to call the authorities. Upon his return, he was horrified to find a second man making love to the corpse.

"*Monsieur,*" he shouted, "that woman is dead!"

"*Sacre bleu!*" the man replied, springing up. "I thought she was an American girl."

A cucumber, a dill pickle, and a penis were sitting around one day, grousing about their lives.

"I hate being a cucumber. They let us grow big and fat and juicy on the vine, then they pick us, peel us, and chop us up to go on some salad, then they eat us."

"At least that's quick," the pickle said. "They let us grow up fat and juicy like you, then they drown us in a vat of vinegar and garlic and spices for months on end before they eat us."

"You guys don't know what torture is," the penis said.

"They let me grow and get big and fat and juicy, then they put a plastic baggy over my head, shove me in a dark, smelly, wet cave, and make me do push-ups until I puke."

Three vampires made their way to their favorite cafe shortly after sunset. The bartender greeted them, then asked what they'd like.

"Something hearty and full blooded, like a deep ruby Burgundy," the first said.

"I'd like something spicier," the second said. "Bring me a Bloody Mary."

The bartender turned to the third vampire. "What'll you have, Count?" he asked.

"Just a cup of hot water," the vampire replied, pulling out a used tampon from his jacket. "I'm going to make tea."

After months of working on a drill rig in the middle of the desert, the three men were wild for female company. On their first trip into town, they managed to lure a young veiled female into the darkness behind their hotel. Unfortunately, they were interrupted by the fierce Arab police, who hauled them in front of the local sheik.

"Infidel dogs," the sheik cursed. "You know what the penalty is for touching a woman of the faith. You will spend the rest of your lives squatting to piss, like a woman."

The three men begged for mercy. The stone-faced sheik ignored their pleas. He slapped the first man across the face and asked, "What is the profession of your father, swine?"

"He's . . . he's a lumberjack," the man stammered.

"You've disgraced him," the sheik said. "So your penis will be chopped off by an ax."

He turned to the second man and asked the same question. The man tried not to answer, but after some persuasion replied, "My father was a fireman."

"Then we will burn your prick off, dog," the sheik said as the man screamed and struggled.

The sheik turned to the third man and was surprised to see a huge grin on his face. "Why are you laughing, swine?" the sheik demanded.

"My father made lollipops!" the man exclaimed.

Milly was in a terrible rush to dress before the dinner party. In desperation, she enlisted the aid of her very reluctant young son to make the salad. She came back down from dressing just in time to find the little rascal pouring a package of BBs over the finished product.

She smacked him good, sent him to his room, then started to pick the little metal balls out of the lettuce. However, her guests arrived, and she had to serve the salad. Fortunately, there were no complaints.

The next day, she couldn't resist calling her friend Nancy, who had been at the dinner, to explain what the boy had done. "Isn't it a miracle no one noticed?" she asked.

"I didn't notice last night," Nancy said. "But I wish you'd told me."

"Why?"

"This morning I bent over, farted, and shot the canary!"

God decided to pay a visit to the Garden of Eden. He soon spotted Adam sitting in the shade eating some fruit. "How's everything going?" God asked.

"Terrific," Adam replied.

"And that woman I made from your rib," God said, "I was worried about how she turned out. Is she satisfactory?"

"No complaints," Adam said. "But she's not here now."

God replied, "I saw her bathing in the stream."

Suddenly Adam started to scowl. "Damn!"

"What's wrong?" God asked.

"Now I suppose all the fish will start smelling like that."

Judy was increasingly frustrated over her inability to excite her husband sexually. In desperation, she confided in her next door neighbor, who asked Judy to describe what happened when they went to bed.

"Bill gets in bed and watches Johnny Carson," Judy said. "I go into the bathroom, wash up, and slip into my nightgown."

"Describe the nightgown."

"It's white, with a high lace front and low cut in back. Bill used to think it was sexy."

"Maybe he just needs a little change," the neighbor

said. "Tonight, why don't you turn it around so it's low in front. That'll turn him on."

Judy agreed. She could barely contain her excitement until her husband climbed into bed. She went into the bathroom and emerged with the nightgown on backwards. She moved seductively across the room, turned off Johnny Carson, turned some soft music on the tape player, got into bed, and nibbled on her husband's ear.

Bill, however, just grunted and rolled over. "Bill!" she screamed. "Why won't you make love to me? Don't you notice anything different about my nightgown?"

"Yeah," he mumbled. "The shit stains are on the front."

The old black drunk was rummaging through a garbage can when he came upon an old lamp. He started rubbing it to see if it was worth anything. Suddenly, the lamp emitted a poof of smoke and a genie appeared.

The black guy stared for a moment, then he said, "Hot dog! I knew I'd find me some luck. Now I get three wishes."

"No you don't," the genie said. "I can only give you two wishes."

"Two? Why you jive-ass, motherfucker," the drunk roared. "I know how this shit works. You gotta give me three, honky shithead."

The genie glared at him. "Listen, man. Count your blessings. You want the wishes or not?"

The black dude grumbled and swore, but finally said, "All right, turdface. At my age, I don't get much luck finding some. I want to be white, and I want to be surrounded by pussy all the time."

"You got it, brother," the genie said. "Poof—you're a tampon."

A farmer and his daughter were driving into town to sell some piglets. They sold the animals, bought a sack of flour, and started back home. They had a flat tire on the way. As the farmer was changing it, a car screeched to a halt. Two men jumped up and robbed them, taking everything including the farmer's watch.

"We're ruined," the farmer wailed.

"No, we're not," his daughter said. "I stuffed the pig money up my cunt."

"It's too bad your mother didn't come," the farmer said. "Then we wouldn't have lost the sack of flour, either."

"Doctor," the man said frantically into the phone, "I've got a problem. My wife was lying in bed nude with her legs wide open and a mouse ran up into her cunt."

"I'll be right there," the doctor said. "But for now, wave a piece of cheese outside the hole. Maybe the mouse will run out."

The man said he'd follow the advice. But when the doctor got there, the man was waving a flounder between his wife's legs. "What are you doing?" the doctor yelled. "Mice don't like fish."

"Mice, hell," the man replied. "Before we get the mouse, we've got to get the cat out of there."

A man was walking down the street when he was smacked in the face by an object thrown from a window. Furious, he pounded on the door until a man answered.

"Who's in the bedroom?" he asked.

"My daughter," the man said.

"And who's with her?"

"My future son-in-law."

The man pulled a dripping wet condom from behind his back and said, "Well, you better get up there. Because I just got hit in the face with your future grandchild."

Two guys just got their drinks in a bar when one held up his glass and said, "You ever see an ice cube with a hole in it?"

"Yeah," the other guy replied. "I've been married to one for twenty-two years."

A man went to the doctor for a physical. Noticing the patient's dark brown balls, the doctor asked the man where he'd gotten such a pair.

The man said, "Just finish your examination."

"I'll examine you for free if you tell me," the doctor said.

"I'll pay."

"I'll pay you $100," the doctor offered.

The man was so angry he got up and left. When he got home he was still mad. He shouted to his wife, "This place is a mess. The kitchen is full of dirty dishes, the bedroom's full of dirty clothes, and the kids are filthy."

She yelled back, "You could help me sometimes. I'm so busy I don't have time to wipe my ass."

"That's another thing I want to talk to you about," the man said.

A man in a hurry goes into a restaurant and orders a bowl of soup. As the waiter serves the soup, the man notices he has two fingers in the bowl. Being in a hurry, the man doesn't say anything, he just eats the soup and leaves.

The man comes back the next day and orders soup. Again, he notices the same waiter has the same two fingers in the soup. "Why the hell can't you keep your fingers out of my lunch?" the man asks.

The waiter replies, "The doctor told me to keep these fingers warm."

"Well, why the hell don't you shove them up your ass?"

The waiter says, "When I go into the kitchen, I do."

A city boy visiting the country decided he wanted to go hunting. He borrowed a shotgun and some shells from his host and started to walk. A ways down the road, he came upon a farmer. He got permission from the farmer to hunt on his lands, as long as he didn't kill any farm animals. Sometime later, he shot a goat. Not knowing what it was he killed, he rushed back to the farmhouse. "Describe the kill," the farmer said.

"It had two tits, a hard head, and a stinking ass."

"Oh, no," the farmer said. "You shot my wife."

A coed was walking across campus when a man leaped out of the bushes, grabbed her, and proceeded to rape her. She struggled for a while, then shouted, "What's the matter, you pervert? Don't you believe in foreplay?"

The farmer had a prize bull. One morning he discovered the bull had crossed eyes, so he summoned the vet. The doc stuck a glass tube up the bull's asshole, blew hard, and the bull's eyes uncrossed.

A few days later, just before the big show at the State Fair, the bull's eyes crossed again. The farmer fetched his hired hand and said, "You watch the bull's eyes." He then put a stiff tube up the bull's asshole and blew on it. But nothing happened.

The farmer then said to the hand, "Here. You blow on it and I'll watch."

The hired hand started to remove the tube. "What in the hell are you pulling that out for?" the farmer demanded.

"You don't think I'm going to blow on the same end as you, do you?" the hand replied.

Two drunks were lying alongside the curb when a cop came up. The officer saw that one had his finger stuck up the other's ass.

"What do you think you're doing?" the cop demanded.

"My buddy is sick and I'm trying to make him throw up," the drunk slurred.

"Well, how the hell is sticking your finger up his ass

going to make him throw up?" the cop asked.

"Just wait," the drunk said, "until I stick it in his mouth."

What's the difference between a prophylactic and a parachute?

When a parachute fails, somebody dies.

What's the height of nerve?

Shitting on a man's doorstep, then ringing the bell and asking for toilet paper.

After several hours at the bar, two men began arguing whose wife was uglier. The debate got heated, and they decided to examine the contestants.

At the first house, the man summoned his wife, and despite their drunkenness, both men recoiled. "Do I win?" the first man asked.

The other man just shook his head and gestured for the first man to follow him. When they got to his house, it was empty. The second man shoved a table out of the way, then asked his guest to assist him in moving a chest. Under the chest was a trap door. The house owner lifted the door and yelled into the darkness, "Stella, come up here a minute."

A voice from below replied, "Should I put on the sack?"

"No," the man replied. "I don't want to screw you. I just want to show you to my buddy."

A man died and went to hell. The devil met him and told him that he could have his choice of three rooms for his punishment. In the first room, a gang of people were walking on hot coals.

"This isn't for me," the man said right away.

They walked into the second room, where a group was lying on beds of nails. "No way," the man said.

In the third room, a smaller group were standing up to their knees in shit. The man thought for a moment, then said, "Of all the rooms, I think I could take this best."

"You're sure?" the devil asked.

"Positive," the man replied, stepping in the room.

"Okay," the devil called out. "Break is over. Everybody back on their heads."

The young couple retired to the room to make love, but she was so tight that he couldn't get in. "Rummage in my bag," she said, "I've got a jar of Vasoline in there."

Without turning on the lights, the man did as requested, and they made passionate love and fell asleep. When the man woke up, however, he was shocked to find that the head of his penis had fallen off. "My God!" he screamed. "What happened?"

"You dunce," the girl said, picking up a jar. "You

didn't get the Vasoline last night. You grabbed my corn remover!"

A man was driving in the country with a young lady. He pulled over to the side and started to reach under her dress. "No," she said. "We can't do it. I'm having my period."

The man grunted and drove on. A little later he pulled over again and began to caress the girl's ass. "No," she said, "we can't do it that way, either. I've got piles."

The man groaned again and drove on. A third time he pulled over, jumped out of the car, grabbed a large stone, and held it up in the air as he unbuttoned his pants. "If you tell me you've got lockjaw," he warned, "I'm going to bash your brains in."

The couple was writhing in bed when he begged her to spread her legs wider. She obliged, but still he urged, "Spread them wider. Oh, just a little wider."

Exasperated, she said, "What in the hell are you trying to do, get your balls in?"

"No," he replied. "I'm trying to get them out."

A man came into a drug store and complained to the owner that he'd broken through every brand of condoms he'd ever tried. The druggist recommended a new brand, but the next day the man glumly reported another failure. The druggist suggested the man wear two at once, then three, then four, but they were no more effective than one.

Finally, the druggist purchased an old rubber raincoat and fashioned a condom out of six layers. He sent the man off, and was severely disappointed when the man failed to reappear. But two days later, he ran into the man on the street.

"What happened?" the druggist asked.

"I've decided to have a baby," the man said glumly. "The damn thing held, all right, but when I came, the recoil almost blew my balls off."

A man walked into a bar and announced that he'd bet anybody in the house that he could correctly identify the brand, vintage, and year of any beverage. The challenge produced several eager bettors. The man was soon blindfolded and handed a glass of clear liquid. He rolled a little around on his tongue, then announced, "Vodka. Smirnoff's."

He immediately collected $20, and soon made another $100 by correctly naming two red wines, a champagne, and a Greek brandy. "Anybody else?" the still-blindfolded man arrogantly challenged. "Or are you all cowed?"

"I'll make you a bet," the bartender replied. "For $200."

The man eagerly accepted. The bartender motioned to a couple cronies to follow him into the back room, then emerged a few minutes later with a glass that he handed to the blindfolded man.

The man sipped, then spat in disgust, "Yuch. That's piss."

"Yeah," the bartender said. "But whose?"

A man spent the night at the home of some friends. In the middle of the night he had to take a shit, but the bathroom was through his host's bedroom and he didn't want to disturb them. Instead, he rummaged through the closet, took a dump in a hat box, then put it back, thinking he'd dispose of the waste the next day. But in the morning he forgot, and he was soon on his way.

A week later, when he returned home, he found waiting a telegram that read, "ALL IS FORGIVEN. BUT WHERE THE HELL IS IT?"

Why do women like Pac-Man so much?

It's the only game where they get eaten three times for a quarter.

An old Indian was sitting in a bar when a long haired, bearded, dirty biker stormed into the bar and ordered a drink. The biker's raunchy insults drove everyone else out of the bar, but the old man sat calmly watching. Finally, the biker turned to him and said, "Hey, redman, why the fuck are you staring at me? You crazy or something?"

"No," the Indian replied. "Twenty years ago I was arrested for fucking a buffalo. I thought you might be my son."

Two unemployed women were discussing the sad state of the economy. "Things are so bad," one said tearfully, "that I let a guy fuck me for $5 last night so I could get a cab home."

"That's nothing," the other said sourly. "I blew a guy for free last night so I could have something warm in my stomach."

The young, naive farm boy was about to be married and he was very nervous. Finally, he asked Zeke, an old farm hand, what he should do on his wedding night. The old man puffed on his pipe a few minutes, then asked, "Boy, you seen dogs go at it in the yard?"

The young man replied that he had.

"Well, then," Zeke continued, "you just do what they do."

The wedding ceremony was the next day, and the couple went off to a motel. But shortly after dawn the mother of the bride was shocked to find her daughter at her door.

"What's wrong?" the mother asked.

"I never want to see that weirdo again in my life," the daughter said angrily.

"Did he make love to you too roughly?" the mother asked.

"He didn't make love at all," the daughter snapped. "He spent the entire night sniffing my asshole and pissing on the bedpost."

An executive walked into a bar and sat down next to a drunk who was studying something in his hand. The executive leaned closer as the drunk held the object up to the light. "Well, it looks like plastic," the drunk said. Then he rolled it around in his fingers, adding, "And it feels like rubber."

Curious, the executive asked, "What do you have there?"

The drunk shook his head. "Damned if I know. It looks like plastic and it feels like rubber."

The executive said, "Let me take a look." The drunk handed it over, examined it, rolled it between his fingers, and commented. "Yeah, you're right. It does look like plastic and feel like rubber. But I don't know what it is. Where did you get it?"

The drunk replied, "Out of my nose."

Two Poles were standing on a Warsaw street corner, each bragging about how smart he was. Finally, one of them said to the other, "I am so smart I can tell if a woman is wearing panties or not, even under a skirt."

"Ridiculous!" the other scoffed. "Nobody's that smart."

"I'll show you," the man said. Soon a woman in her thirties walked by. "There," the man said. "She's not wearing panties."

The two men walked up to the woman. "We've got a big bet going," they said. "You've got to tell us if you're wearing panties or not."

The woman was shocked, but the men finally convinced her to talk. After a little stammering, she confessed she was pantyless.

"How did you know?" the incredulous challenger asked.

"Easy," came the reply. "She had dandruff on her shoes."

What do you call the dirt in the bottom of a woman's underwear?

Clitty litter.

The tradition in one military regiment was to screw women when they were having their period. The reason was that a good soldier should always be ready to prove his willingness to fight through blood to glory.

The couple were driving along in the mountains when the woman asked the man to stop the car so she could take a shit. He pulled over a little while later and told her to shit over the edge of a cliff.

She complied. A few moments later, she called out,

"George. Come here. I'm afraid I shit into a canoe down below."

He came running over and peered down. "You idiot," he said. "That's not a canoe. It's a reflection of your cunt."

Two baseball outfielders had been conversing for innings about a rather well built young lady whose legs were invitingly spread apart. The woman had bright red hair on her head, but her cunt was deep black.

In the fifth inning, a deep fly ball took the left fielder to the wall just below the woman. He caught the ball, ending the inning. As the outfielders jogged to the dugout, he said to his buddy, "Forget that broad."

"Why?"

"In the excitement of that catch, she jumped to her feet. I could see that wasn't black hair covering her crotch—it was flies."

A male leper came into the infirmary of the leper colony and saw his friend George sitting in the chair grinning from ear to ear as the doctor bandaged the bleeding stump of his right hand.

"What happened?" the man asked. "Why are you grinning like that when all your fingers are gone?"

"You know I've been looking to marry that blonde in the female colony?"

"What does that have to do with your fingers?"

"Well," the leper said with a smile. "I wanted to know

if I should ask her to marry me. So I started pulling at my fingers. She loves me, she loves me not, she loves me . . ."

How do they punish patients in a leper colony?

They make them do jumping jacks until something falls off.

How can you tell a letter is from the leper colony?

Because a tongue is stuck to the stamp.

Why did Helen Keller lose her secret pen pal?

Because she wrote all her letters in invisible braille.

What's the definition of endless love?

Ray Charles and Helen Keller playing tennis.

When did Helen Keller's parents decide she needed psychiatric care?

When they caught her turning on the stereo and flipping on the lights.

What did Helen Keller get for her birthday?

Polio.

What's the definition of a tampon?

A beaver dam.

What's the favorite fastfood dish in Transylvania?

A tampon pizza.

The female executive came back from the convention only to discover she was pregnant. She told a friend about her condition, complaining, "I can't believe this. I made my computations, and I only had a 16% chance to get pregnant."

"Is that the failure rate for IUDs?" her friend asked.

"I wasn't using an IUD," the pregnant woman replied.

"I got drunk at the convention and ended up playing Sperm Roulette."

"What's Sperm Roulette?" the puzzled friend asked.

"That's where you get to choose one of six shooters, and only five of them have had vasectomies."

A very well dressed man walked into the bordello and told the madam he was incredibly horny. "I want a girl who will do absolutely everything I ask," the man said. "And I'll pay $1000 for the privilege."

At that price, several girls jumped forward. The man selected a tall blonde, took her upstairs, handed her the money, then started in. First he pissed on her, then he shat on her, then he whipped her endlessly with a thick belt. After a while, the poor girl screamed, "I can't take much more. When are you going to quit?"

"I'm almost done," the man replied. "I've only got one more demand."

"Anything," the half-dead girl stammered.

"Give me my $1000 back."

The cannibal chief entered the village, only to see two men burying a missionary alive.

"Hey," the chief called out. "Why are you throwing out perfectly good food?"

"Good food, hell," one man replied. "This guy's rotten to the core. We no sooner started the fire then he shit in the pot and ruined our lunch."

What's the difference between a shipment of fertilizer and the cheeks of your ass?

Nothing. You can get the same smell spreading either one.

How does a hillbilly wipe his ass?

First he pulls up the front of his overalls, then the back, then the front, then the back . . .

The young widow went to the undertaker to make funeral arrangements. The funeral director said, "I understand everything but this last request. Why do you want your husband buried so that his bare ass is sticking up out of the ground."

"That's simple," the girl said. "When I come to visit his grave, I want some place to park my bicycle."

A man on a picnic had to take a dump, so he headed into the bushes. He had barely dropped his trousers when a young lady stood up from behind a bush and asked, "Hey, there, big guy. Can I take advantage of you?"

"Sure," he replied eagerly.

So she leaned over, grabbed his shirttail and wiped her ass with it.

Why couldn't Lois Lane get an abortion?

The fetus kept smashing the doctor's tools.

Why did the hunchback have to file for unemployment?

Because there aren't many jobs for camel impersonators.

Why did the bishop write a recommendation for the hunchback to work on a construction crew?

He automatically wrote a recommendation for every Notre Dame man.

ZEBRA BRINGS YOU EXCITING BESTSELLERS
by Lewis Orde

MUNICH 10 (1300, $3.95)

They've killed her lover, and they've kidnapped her son. Now the world-famous actress is swept into a maelstrom of international intrigue and bone-chilling suspense—and the only man who can help her pursue her enemies is a complete stranger . . . .

HERITAGE (1100, $3.75)

Beautiful innocent Leah and her two brothers were forced by the holocaust to flee their parents' home. A courageous immigrant family, each battled for love, power and their very lifeline—their HERITAGE.

THE LION'S WAY (900, $3.75)

An all-consuming saga that spans four generations in the life of troubled and talented David, who struggles to rise above his immigrant heritage and rise to a world of glamour, fame and success!

Available wherever paperbacks are sold, or order direct from the Publisher. Send cover price plus 50¢ per copy for mailing and handling to Zebra Books, 475 Park Avenue South, New York, N.Y. 10016. DO NOT SEND CASH.